# The Art of Living Fully After Success

## RECLAIM DESIRE, FREEDOM, AND AUTHORITY WITHOUT GUILT

Maria L. Ellis, BBA, MBA

**Ellis Publishing House**
Washington, DC, USA



First Edition Published: 2026

## DISCLAIMER



Cover Design: Jennifer Stimson
Editing: Cory Hott

# DEDICATION

For the women who came before us
who endured quietly, who built steadily,
who held families and futures together with hands no
one applauded.
For the mothers who gave more than they kept.
For the daughters who learned strength by watching.
For the women who achieved what was required
and are now brave enough to ask what is true.
For the daughters and granddaughters who are
watching
how we age, how we speak, how we choose
ourselves.
May they inherit not only what we built,
but the courage with which we lived.
May they see women who did not disappear after
success,
who did not shrink to make others comfortable,
who did not confuse guilt with goodness.
And to every seasoned woman standing at the
threshold of "What now?"
this book is for you!

# TABLE OF CONTENTS

# FOREWORD

## *The Art of Living Fully After Success:*
## *How Seasoned Women Reclaim Desire,*
## *Freedom, and Authority Without Guilt*

## by Maria L. Ellis, BBA, MBA

There is a quiet moment that arrives in the life of a seasoned woman—a moment that few speak about openly. This book voices that moment with unflinching tenderness and quiet courage. It invites us to name what many carry in the shadows: the realization that achievement, once the north star, can become a border we outgrow.

Maria L. Ellis does not offer a new formula for success. She offers something rarer: a pathway to integration. Not reinvention for applause, but a sustainable alignment of what we have earned with what we now long to be. She writes for the woman who has exhausted the currency of productivity and wonder whether there could be a different measure—the one that honors rest as intelligence, and power as responsibility, not performance.

What makes this work so essential is its cadence. It speaks from lived experience—an economy of action that understands cost and consequence, triumph and tenderness. It honors ambition while revealing its cost when it is unmoored from inner authority. In these pages, autonomy does not fracture; it deepens. Rest is not weakness; it is a form of clarity. Intimacy does not require performance; it requires presence. Authority does not demand apology; it asks for coherence.

Maria does not deny the pull of a life that has already proven itself. She invites us to attend to the next season—the one where desire can become direction, not indulgence; where freedom is not rebellion but responsibility, where leadership is grounded in alignment rather than output. The book offers both language and space for that shift—a permission slip to want again, to take up space, to lead with steadiness and grace.

If you have walked the path of high achievement and

sensed that something essential is shifting, this book will feel like a conversation with your own interior compass. It does not demand that you erase who you have been; it asks you to steward who you are becoming. The art here is not loud. It is deliberate. It is sovereign.

May these pages meet you where you stand and carry you toward a life of deep coherence—where fulfillment rests not on the applause of others, but on the quiet alignment you author within yourself. Enjoy every chapter and please don't forget to do the exercises that close out each section…

Lynne DuVivier, Entrepreneur & Mentor

# INTRODUCTION

There was a morning not long ago when I woke up and realized that nothing was urgent. No children needed to be driven anywhere. No deadlines pressed against the edges of the day.

No crisis required my steady hand. For decades, my life had been organized around responsibility, building businesses, raising a family, supporting others, showing up with strength even when I was tired. I wore competence like a well-tailored jacket. It fit. It worked. It earned respect.

And yet, on that quiet morning, something unfamiliar stirred. It was not dissatisfaction. It was not regret. It was not even exhaustion. It was space. And in that space, a question rose that no achievement had prepared me to answer: If I no longer need to prove anything… who am I now?

I had spent years helping others build, grow, succeed, and recover after setbacks. I knew how to set goals, how to endure, how to lead. What I had not fully practiced was how to arrive. How to live without bracing. How to choose without guilt. How to rest without negotiating my worth.

Success has given me freedom. But freedom required a different kind of courage. The courage to stop performing competence. The courage to feel desire without justification. The courage to tell the truth about what no longer fit. That is where this book began, not in crisis, but in clarity.

There comes a moment, often after success, achievement, and decades of responsibility, when life no longer asks us to prove anything. Instead, it asks us to listen. To feel. To align. To tell the truth about what brings aliveness now.

For many women, that moment arrives quietly. The roles have been fulfilled. The ladders climbed. The obligations are honored. And yet, beneath the surface of accomplishment, a deeper question emerges: Who am I now, beyond what I've done?

## Why This Book Exists Now

This book was not written to teach, persuade, or correct. It was written because a truth kept asking to be named.

This book was born from that question.

We live in a culture that celebrates striving but rarely teaches us how to arrive. That praises women for endurance, sacrifice, and usefulness, yet grows uneasy when they choose freedom, pleasure, or rest without apology. The seasoned woman stands at the intersection of these tensions, not because she is confused, but because she has outgrown the old terms of engagement.

This is not a book about aging as decline. It is a book about maturation as power. It is written for women who have lived long enough to know that success does not guarantee fulfillment, that love without boundaries exhausts, that achievement without alignment empties the body, and that worth was never meant to be earned through effort alone.

It is also written for the men who love them, work beside them, and grow with them, men who recognize the steady strength of a woman who no longer feels the need to prove her worth.

What follows is a constellation of reflections, truths, and lived recognitions. You will find yourself in some chapters more than others. You may feel relief, resistance, or quiet recognition. All are welcome. This book does not rush you. It trusts your timing.

If you are reading this in a season of transition, uncertainty, or quiet dissatisfaction, know this: nothing is wrong with you. You are not late. You are not ungrateful. You are not losing relevance. You are refining your relationship with life.

The second half of life is not an afterthought. It is an initiation. And the seasoned woman is not stepping away from meaning – she is stepping into authorship.

May these pages offer you permission rather than instruction. Language rather than pressure. Companionship rather than answers. And may you feel, as you read, that you are not alone in choosing alignment over obligation, presence over performance, and aliveness over approval.

This book exists because enough women are ready to live that choice out loud.

With respect and recognition,
Maria L. Ellis, BBA, MBA

# CHAPTER 1:
# THE UNSPOKEN
# EXPERIENCE OF SUCCESS

*'The most difficult thing is the decision to act;
the rest is merely tenacity.'*

— Amelia Earhart

I sat alone in my car for a moment longer than necessary, the engine already off, my hand resting on the steering wheel.

The parking garage carried that familiar scent of concrete dust and faint motor oil – cool, mineral, slightly metallic. Somewhere above me, a car door slammed and footsteps echoed in hollow rhythm against cement. The fluorescent lights hummed softly, casting everything in a pale, unflattering glow. It was midafternoon, but down here it could have been any hour.

On the radio, a news anchor's voice spoke steadily about markets and policy shifts – measured, confident, urgent in tone but emotionally neutral. I reached forward and lowered the volume until it became background murmur, then turned it off entirely. The sudden quiet felt thicker than the sound.

The meeting had gone well – productive, respectful,

efficient. I had said what needed to be said. I had been heard. I had been thanked. Nothing lingered unnamed.

My leather seat still held the warmth of my body. The folder beside me – neatly organized, color-tabbed – was closed, complete. My phone screen lit up briefly with a new notification, then dimmed again when I didn't reach for it.

I stared at the faint reflection of myself in the windshield. Not studying. Not critiquing. Just noticing.

The posture of composure was still in place – shoulders squared, chin level, breath steady. A lifetime of showing up prepared.

And yet, I did not immediately open the door.

My fingers remained curved around the steering wheel, as if I were still driving, still navigating, still responsible for direction. I became aware of the subtle indentation the wheel had left against my palm. A small imprint. Temporary, but real.

There was no disappointment. No visible failure. No conflict replaying itself in my mind. By every professional measure, it had been a success.

Still, I remained seated.

Not because something had gone wrong.

But because something inside me was asking for a moment of honesty before I stepped back into motion.

In that dim garage, between accomplishment and arrival, I felt the quiet weight of being the steady one. The composed one. The capable one.

The one who holds the room together.

And for just a breath longer than necessary, I allowed myself to feel what it costs to do that well.

I had said what needed to be said. I had been heard. I had been thanked. Nothing lingered unnamed.

As I reached for my bag, a familiar thought surfaced, uninvited and unresolved.

Is this it?

It was not a question born of dissatisfaction or regret. There was no crisis waiting for me inside the building or at home. My life worked. It functioned smoothly. People depended on me. I was good at what I did. And yet something in me hesitated – not forward, not backward, just suspended.

I noticed how easily I moved through my days, how practiced my competence had become. I knew what was expected of me and how to deliver it. I knew how to be reliable, capable, and strong. What I no longer knew, at least not clearly, was how to locate myself inside all of it.

Later that evening, after the house had gone quiet, I sat with a cup of tea I did not really want, scrolling absently, avoiding the pull of my thoughts. The feeling returned – not loud, not urgent, just present. A sense that a chapter had ended without ceremony. That I had crossed an invisible threshold without being told there would be questions on the other side.

I did not feel ungrateful.

I felt unfinished.

There is a particular kind of loneliness that often accompanies success, and it is rarely spoken about openly. It does not come from isolation or lack of connection. It comes from being relied upon, admired, and respected, yet still not fully seen or known for who you truly are. It comes from having achieved what once felt essential, only to realize, quietly and sometimes uncomfortable, that the inner questions did not disappear when the milestones were reached.

They simply became more private.

I remember mentioning this to my friend Connie over lunch one afternoon at the Harvard Club in New York City. We were seated near the window, we both loved, sunlight catching the rim of our glasses, the steady hum of conversation around us.

"You ever feel," I began carefully, tracing the edge of my napkin, "like everyone assumes you're fine because you've handled everything so well?"

Connie didn't answer immediately. She leaned back

slightly and studied the way only an old friend can – without interruption, without performance.

"You mean," she said gently, "like they see your strength, but not the weight of it?"

I exhaled before I realized I was holding my breath.

"Yes," I said. "Exactly that."

She nodded, not with surprise, but with recognition.

"Maria, you've been the capable one for so long," she continued. "People don't think to ask how you're really doing. They assume if something were wrong, you'd fix it."

We both laughed softly, not because it was amusing, but because it was true.

"That's the irony," I said. "There's nothing wrong. I'm grateful. I'm proud. I'm deeply aware of the blessings. And yet…" I paused, searching for language that did not sound ungrateful. "There are still questions."

"What kind of questions?" she asked.

"The kind that don't fit into a quarterly plan," I replied. "The kind that don't show up on an award. The kind that asks who I am now, not what I've built."

Connie reached the table and rested her hand over mine.

"That's not loneliness," she said quietly. "That's evolution."

Her words stayed with me.

Because what we rarely admit is this: success changes the questions, but it does not eliminate them. It shifts the terrain from proving to becoming. From achieving to aligning.

And if we are not careful, we can mistake that shift for dissatisfaction, when it is actually maturation.

The seasoned woman does not ache for more applause. She aches for deeper truth. She does not want another ladder. She wants coherence.

That afternoon Connie did not solve anything. It did something better. It named the experience.

And once named, it could no longer be dismissed as

weakness.

It was not a lack of gratitude.

It was not restlessness.

It was not decline.

It was the quiet realization that being respected is not the same as being revealed.

This loneliness is subtle. It hides beneath productivity and competence. It lives under calendars filled and roles fulfilled. From the outside, I appeared steady, accomplished, and self-assured. From the inside, I felt a growing distance between how I was perceived and how I experienced my life.

Like many women, I arrived at the second half of life with a full life. A career built. A family raised. Responsibilities carried for decades. Communities served. Problems solved. People supported. There was evidence of contribution everywhere – résumés, photographs, plaques on the wall, framed certificates marking years of achievement.

And yet inside, something felt unresolved. Not broken. Not dramatic. Not in crisis. Just quietly unfinished.

This book begins there.

For me, the disorientation did not arrive at a single moment. It unfolded gradually, often during periods of relative calm. The urgency that once drove my decisions softened. The pace changed. And in that softening, questions surfaced, not loudly, but persistently.

What once motivated me now felt hollow. What once felt urgent now felt strangely distant. The old measures of success no longer carried the same authority, even though they had once served me well.

This was not boredom. It was not ingratitude. It was not failure. It was grief.

I did not recognize it at first because it did not look like grief. There was no singular loss I could point to, no event that would have justified stopping. Instead, it moved quietly through ordinary moments.

I noticed it one afternoon while sorting through a drawer I had not opened in years. Inside were remnants of earlier versions of myself – handwritten notes, photographs, business cards embossed with titles I once carried, name badges from conferences long finished. I lingered longer than necessary, not because I wanted to return to those moments, but because I could feel their weight. These lives had been lived fully. They had mattered.

And yet, there was no ritual for setting them down.

What I felt was not longing for the past, but the ache of acknowledging that something had ended without acknowledgment. The woman who once moved through life with urgency and clear ambition was gone, and no one had marked her passing, not even me. I simply kept going.

This grief lived in the body more than the mind. It showed up as fatigue I could not sleep away. As a heaviness that followed accomplishment rather than satisfaction. As a quiet resistance to beginning things that once would have energized me.

I was not sad in the traditional sense. I was subdued, as though a vital current had slowed.

I told myself this was normal. I had earned rest. I had achieved enough. And yet the grief persisted, not because I wanted more, but because something essential had not been named. I had outgrown identities that once gave me structure, but I had not yet claimed what would replace them.

At times, this grief sharpened into irritation. I found myself impatient with small demands, resentful of expectations I had once met without hesitation. The anger surprised me. It felt disproportionate, misdirected. Only later did I understand it as grief's protective edge, the response that arises when loss goes unrecognized.

At other times, the grief flattened instead of sharpened. My days were full yet thin. Decisions were made efficiently, but without resonance. When asked how I was, I answered automatically, fine, busy, good. Alone later, I realized those words no longer connected to anything inside me.

Nothing was wrong. And yet something essential felt muted.

What made this grief especially difficult was that it had no name. There was no socially acceptable language for mourning a self that had evolved. No permission to grieve roles released by choice or necessity rather than tragedy. And so, I minimized it. I told myself it was indulgent. I moved past it quickly, as I had been trained to do.

But grief does not disappear when ignored. It waits.

Empathy matters here because women like me are often rushed past this stage. Encouraged to reframe quickly. To focus on gratitude. While reframing has its place, premature reassurance can feel dismissive. It suggests discomfort is something to fix rather than something to understand.

This chapter is an invitation to pause.

Before solutions. Before strategies. Before reinvention.

Before deciding what comes next, there is value in naming what is true. The exhaustion that comes from being emotionally reliable for decades.

The way desire slowly went quiet under schedules, responsibility, and endless competence. The ache of being recognized primarily for roles rather than wholeness.

I had been praised for being strong. Few had asked how that strength had shaped me. Strength protected me, but it also constrained me. It limited vulnerability. It made rest feel undeserved. It obscured needs that no longer fit the identity I had learned to inhabit.

There was fear at this threshold. Fear of becoming irrelevant. Fear of disappointing others by changing. Fear of discovering that approval had been more conditional than I wanted to believe. These fears arose because my identity had been closely tied to usefulness and contribution.

Feeling these things did not mean I had failed. It meant I was paying attention.

Empathy, in this context, is not pity. It is recognition.

It is the acknowledgment that this stage of life carries both privilege and complexity. That clarity is often preceded by confusion. That growth does not always feel expansive at first. Sometimes it feels like standing in a doorway, knowing you cannot remain where you are – yet unsure what you will have to release to move forward.

This book does not begin by telling you what to do.

It begins by honoring where I was, and where you may be.

You are not behind. You are not broken. You are not ungrateful for noticing that something wants to change. The questions arising now are not a rejection of your past. They are a response to who you have become.

And like the moment I sat in my car before stepping back into that building, it is enough, for now, to stay with the question.

This is where we begin.

## Reflective Questions

1. In what ways has your success complicated your inner life rather than simplified it?

2. What questions have been quietly forming that you have not yet allowed yourself to ask fully?

3. Where do gratitude and grief coexist in your life, and how do you typically respond to that tension?

4. What roles or identities have you outgrown without fully acknowledging the loss they represent?

5. How has being seen as strong shaped what you allow yourself to need, express, or rest from?

6. What feels unfinished, unnamed, or unspoken at this stage of your life?

# CHAPTER 2: MY STORY

*"The most convincing teachers are those*
*who have lived what they speak."*

— Maria L. Ellis

For most of my life, I was defined by what I did. I carried roles that made sense to the world and to me. Professional. Partner. Mother. Leader. Provider. Builder. These identities offered structure and direction. They provided clarity about where I belonged and how I was valued. I was competent, capable, and trusted. I knew how to take responsibility and how to deliver. I understood momentum. I understood how to keep moving, even when the path was demanding.

From the outside, my life looked full and successful. And in many ways, it was.

I had built a career in banking that I was genuinely proud of. Early on, I worked with Bank of America, structuring lines of credit and export financing for Fortune 500 companies exporting goods into Latin America. The transactions were complex, cross-border risk, currency fluctuations, geopolitical considerations. I learned to read balance sheets the way some people read novels. I learned to ask disciplined questions. I learned how to assess financial exposure, structure security, and protect against volatility.

There was satisfaction in that world. Precision mattered. Strategy mattered. Competence was measurable. A deal either closed or it did not. A credit facility either performed or it did not. The clarity was almost comforting.

Later, my work deepened and became more personal. I began helping business owners manage their capital, guiding them through liquidity decisions, succession planning, and the delicate architecture of estate design. These were not just financial conversations; they were conversations about legacy.

I sat across polished conference tables from founders who had built companies from nothing, men and women who had risked everything for an idea. I watched them wrestle with questions that had nothing to do with EBITDA and everything to do with family:

*Will my children be ready?*

*Will the business survive me?*

*How do I protect what I've built without controlling the next generation?*

Together, we created structures, trusts, governance plans, liquidity events, that would outlive them. We translated vision into documentation. We turned decades of labor into intergenerational stability.

From the outside, it looked impressive.

And it was.

I had influence. I had responsibility. I had a seat at tables where consequential decisions were made. I was respected for my clarity, for my discipline, for my steadiness under pressure.

But what is rarely acknowledged is that when you help others build their legacies, you quietly begin to question your own.

When you spend years advising on succession, you eventually ask: *What am I succeeding into?*

When you help others protect what matters most, you

begin to wonder: *What matters most to me now?*

There was no crisis. No dramatic unraveling. Just a subtle shift.

The metrics that once energized me began to feel incomplete. Not irrelevant – just insufficient.

Success had delivered what it promised.

And then it delivered silence.

I contributed meaningfully and consistently. I had shown up for people who depended on me, sometimes quietly, sometimes at great personal cost. I had learned to manage complexity and uncertainty, to make decisions under pressure, and to remain steady when others needed reassurance. These were not illusions. They were real achievements, earned through effort, discipline, and commitment.

And yet, something shifted quietly, long before I had language for it.

The change did not arrive as a crisis or collapse. There was no dramatic rupture, no singular event that forced my attention. Instead, it arrived as a subtle dissonance. The strategies that had once worked felt heavy. The roles that had once energized me asked more than they gave. I noticed a kind of fatigue that rest did not fully resolve, a weariness that sleep alone could not reach. Beneath my outward effectiveness, I sensed that I was performing competence rather than inhabiting it.

What unsettled me most was not exhaustion, but loss of resonance. I could still function. I could still achieve. I could still meet expectations and deliver results. What I could no longer do was pretend that effort alone was enough, or that success automatically produced fulfillment.

There was grief in this realization.

I grieved versions of myself that had been admired and affirmed. I grieved the ease of knowing exactly how to be valued and rewarded. I grieved the sense of forward motion that achievement provides, the reassurance that comes from measurable progress. I grieved identities that had carried me through decades and were now loosening without my consent.

This grief was confusing because nothing was obviously wrong. I had not failed. I had not fallen apart. I had not lost my capacity or my relevance. And yet something essential was ending. A way of being that had once fit no longer did, even though it had served me well.

Of course, I tried to fix it.

I looked for new goals, new projects, and new ways to apply the skills I already had. I stayed productive. I stayed useful. I stayed engaged. I assumed the answer was refinement, redirection, or reinvestment of effort.

If something felt unsettled, I would optimize it.

That had always worked before.

What I did not do, at first, was listen.

The fatigue began subtly. Not dramatic enough to alarm me, not severe enough to interrupt performance. It was simply a dull, persistent heaviness. I could still function. I could still deliver. I could still lead a room without anyone sensing strain.

But when the room emptied, something in me did not refill.

Sleep no longer restored the way it once had. I would wake before dawn – alert but not energized. My shoulders held tension that stretching did not fully release. Even enthusiasm required negotiation.

It was not exhaustion from overwork. I knew that feeling well. This was different.

It was as if my body had begun to withhold its automatic agreement.

I did what competent women do: I scheduled a medical checkup.

The appointment was orderly and uneventful. Blood pressure steady. Lab work thorough. A review of numbers and ranges. I answered questions efficiently, almost reassuringly.

A few days later, the call came.

"Everything looks normal," my doctor said. "Your labs are strong. No signs of concern."

I felt relief.

And then something else.

"If everything is normal," I asked carefully, "why do I feel this tired?"

There was a brief pause on the other end.

"You've had a demanding life," he said. "Stress accumulates. But medically? There's nothing wrong."

Nothing wrong.

It is a powerful phrase.

Nothing broken.

Nothing diagnosable.

Nothing to treat.

I drove home with that sentence echoing quietly.

Nothing wrong.

And yet something was asking to change.

The fatigue was not pathology. It was information.

For decades, I had regulated rooms, absorbed complexity, carried responsibility without visible strain. I had been steady through transitions, composed through negotiations, measured in decision-making. I had learned to metabolize tension quickly and privately.

The body keeps its own accounting.

And mine was presenting a different kind of balance sheet.

Not a deficit of health.

A deficit of alignment.

I began to see that what I had called resilience had, at times, been prolonged self-containment. What I had labeled strength had occasionally required self-silencing. What I had framed as leadership had sometimes meant absorbing emotional weight without redistribution.

No blood test measures that.

No scan reveals the cost of decades spent being the dependable one.

But the body registers everything.

The checkup did not reveal disease. It revealed responsibility.

If nothing was medically wrong, then the invitation was not to fix, but to listen.

To notice where effort had replaced desire.

To notice where obligation had outlived purpose.

To notice where empathy had become endurance.

My body had insisted.

And for the first time in a long while, I stopped trying to override it.

Fatigue became information rather than inconvenience. It was no longer something to push through, but something to listen to.

Desire went quiet, not dramatically, but persistently. Time felt compressed even when my schedule lightened. I noticed how often I was living in response to expectation rather than internal alignment. I could see how easily my energy had been shaped by obligation, by habit, by what I believed I should want rather than what sustained me.

This was not a breakdown.

It was a reckoning.

What emerged slowly was a different kind of attention. I noticed what steadied me rather than what advanced me. I became more interested in what brought clarity than what generated momentum. I valued rest not as recovery for more effort, but as a way of seeing clearer. I started to recognize when something was no longer mine to carry, even if I had carried it well in the past.

I also noticed how difficult it was to stop apologizing for change.

I apologized for slowing down.

I apologized for choosing differently.

I apologized for no longer wanting what I had once wanted.

Those apologies were subtle, sometimes unspoken, but persistent. Letting go of them took time. It required me to question why continuity felt safer than honesty, and why I hesitated to act until someone else confirmed what I already knew.

As I released performance, something else returned.

Presence returned. Discernment returned. Desire returned, not the driven kind fueled by proving, but a quieter, more grounded wanting. Relationships felt more honest, less transactional. Work felt less extractive, less tied to identity and more aligned with contribution. I was not becoming someone new. I was becoming more coherent.

At the same time, I recognized how common this transition is, and how rarely it is named. Women around me were navigating similar shifts quietly. They were accomplished, thoughtful, and often deeply confused by what they were feeling. Many believed they were alone in it. Many assumed they should already have answers, or that their questions were a sign of ingratitude or weakness.

They were not.

Neither was I.

I was not interested in offering solutions. I wanted to tell the truth." Not the dramatic truth of reinvention narratives, but the quieter truth of integration. The truth of listening to the body. The truth of sitting with grief rather than rushing past it. The truth of discovering that authority in the second half of life feels different. It is quieter. It is less defensive. It does not need to be announced or justified.

This book grew from that impulse. Not from theory, but from lived integration. From paying attention. From allowing uncertainty to do its work. From learning that wisdom in this stage of life is less about certainty and more about alignment.

My credibility does not come from having mastered this transition. It comes from having walked it, imperfectly, attentively, and honestly. I am still walking it.

What I know now is this: the second half of life is not decline. It is reorientation. It asks different questions. It rewards different capacities. It invites a woman to live from alignment rather than accumulation — to choose coherence over performance.

I wrote this book because I needed it. And because I could see that others did too.

If you recognize yourself anywhere in these pages, if something in you feels relieved simply by being named, then this work has already begun to do what it was meant to do.

You are not late.

You are not failing.

You are not losing relevance.

You are transitioning.

## Reflective Questions

1. Which roles have defined you most strongly until now, and how have they shaped your sense of self

2. What has quietly begun to feel heavy, constrained, or misaligned in your life

3. What forms of grief have accompanied change, even without obvious loss

4. How has your body been signaling the need for a different way of living or working

5. Where do you notice yourself apologizing for change, rest, or evolving desire

6. What has begun to return as performance has loosened its hold

7. What might become possible if you trusted this transition rather than resisted it?

# CHAPTER 3:
# THE ROAD MAP

*"You do not have to see the whole path
to take the next true step."*

— Maria L. Ellis

Every meaningful journey benefits from orientation. Not to control the experience, but to establish trust. When we understand the general shape of what lies ahead, we can relax into the process rather than brace against it. We stop rushing toward conclusions and allow insight to gather in the body first, in the tightening or softening of a response, before it ever becomes language.

This book is not meant to be consumed quickly or applied mechanically. It is meant to be lived alongside. The chapters are not instructions to follow in sequence. They are invitations to notice where you are and what is asking for attention now. Knowing the terrain allows you to move with greater ease, even when the path curves, pauses, or circles back.

What follows is not a checklist. It is the shape of a journey, one that unfolds in phases rather than steps.

## Identity and Self

The journey begins inward. Before relationships

change or choices shift, identity softens. The roles that once provided clarity loosen. The internal questions introduced in the opening chapters are not problems to solve, but signals of transition.

Chapter 4, *Grief After Success*, gives language to what is often felt but rarely named, the loss that can arrive after achievement, when meaning has not yet caught up with momentum. It honors the quiet grief that can coexist with pride and accomplishment. Grief After Success does not pathologize this moment. It normalizes it. It reframes it as maturation rather than decline, as transition rather than emptiness. Because sometimes the deepest grief is not over what we lost – but over what we outgrew.

Chapter 5, *Receiving Instead of Achieving*, explores what happens when effort no longer leads. It invites a shift from striving to receptivity, from constant doing to allowing. Receiving is named not as passivity, but as a different form of strength that requires trust rather than control.

Together, these chapters establish a foundation. What comes next cannot be built without acknowledging what has ended.

## Relationships

As identity shifts, relationships follow. Patterns once sustained by obligation, performance, or quiet endurance begin to ask for something braver – honesty instead of duty, choice instead of habit, change instead of mere survival. This phase explores connection when women stop organizing their lives around being needed.

Chapter 6, *The Courage to Be Unneeded*, examines what remains when roles loosen and relevance is no longer tied to indispensability.

Chapter 7, *Friendship in the Second Half of Life*, addresses how intimacy deepens when comparison fades and connection is no longer built on shared performance or obligation.

Chapter 8, Visibility Without Performance, Being Seen

Without Proving, invites the reader to consider a quieter, more grounded form of visibility that arises from alignment rather than effort.

Chapter 9, *Love Without Obligation*, reframes autonomy and boundaries as strengthening forces rather than threats to intimacy, inviting love that is chosen freely rather than maintained through sacrifice or duty.

Chapter 10, *Intimacy and Desire*, restores desire by removing performance and reestablishing safety, honesty, and presence.

Chapter 11, *Money and Power in Partnership*, addresses money as a relational language, exploring power without domination and contribution without control.

Chapter 12, *When Choosing Yourself Disrupts the Room*, explores what happens when growth meets resistance — when partners, children, or friends struggle to adjust to the woman you are becoming. It names the friction, normalizes the pushback, and offers grounding for staying true without losing compassion.

Chapter 13, *Why Men Thrive Beside a Seasoned Woman*, examines how men respond when the women in their lives stop performing, rescuing, and shrinking — and how partnerships often deepen when coherence replaces accommodation.

This phase asks a central question. What becomes possible in relationship when you no longer abandon yourself to remain connected.

## Body and Time

With relational patterns examined, the journey turns toward the body and the lived experience of time, often where women report the greatest relief.

Chapter 14, *Rest as Intelligence*, reframes rest as wisdom rather than weakness and invites the body back into decision making.

Chapter 15, *Aliveness in the Presence of Loss*, addresses what this season also includes — illness, physical limitation, caregiving, and mortality – and explores how aliveness remains possible not by denying loss, but by staying present within it.

Chapter 16, *The Nervous System Knows*, grounds these shifts in physiology, showing how regulation restores clarity, connection, and choice.

Chapter 17, *The Body as Ally*, acknowledges physical change, illness, loss, and mortality without surrendering vitality, restoring the body as a source of information rather than a problem to solve.

Chapter 18, *Time Reclaimed*, releases urgency and invites a different way of inhabiting time, one rooted in presence rather than pressure.

Here, the question becomes. What changes when you stop overriding your body and begin trusting its intelligence.

## Presence and Freedom

As internal authority strengthens, aging itself becomes a site of liberation rather than diminishment.

Chapter 19, *Aging Without Apology, Releasing Shame and Trusting Yourself*, focuses on the internal shift away from self-diminishment as external validation loses authority.

Chapter 20, *Voice, Visibility, and Beauty Redefined*, explores how that internal shift changes presence, expression, and self-regard.

Chapter 21, *The Wisdom of Timing*, honors discernment, knowing when to act, when to wait, and when to let go.

Chapter 22, *Living with Enough*, releases scarcity mindset and allows sufficiency to register not as compromise, but as freedom.

Chapter 23, *Mentorship Without Control*, reframes influence as generosity rather than ownership, offering guidance without attachment to outcome.

This phase asks. What becomes possible when you no longer need to prove your worth to occupy space.

## Legacy

As the book closes, the lens widens beyond the personal contribution and meaning.

Chapter 24, *The Feminine as Stabilizer*, names the feminine not as a role, but as a way of being – steady, relational, and coherent in unstable systems.

Chapter 25, *Where You Begin*, meets the reader in the practical reality of a life still full of obligations. It offers a compassionate guide to what the first week, month, and season of choosing yourself might actually look like – not as a dramatic overhaul, but as a series of small, honest experiments.

Chapter 26, *The Quiet Revolution*, brings the journey to arrival, not as an ending, but as a way of living. Presence over proving. Alignment over approval. Coherence over performance.

Chapter 27, *Legacy – Joy, Abundance, and What We Leave Behind*, explores how the choices made in this season ripple forward – through joy modeled rather than prescribed, abundance shared rather than hoarded, and values transmitted through how we live rather than what we leave.

This road map is not meant to rush you forward. You may recognize yourself more strongly in later chapters than earlier ones. You may circle back. That is intentional. Growth is not linear. It unfolds in seasons.

You are not being asked to become someone else. You are invited to live as yourself with less apology, less urgency, and greater coherence.

Take your time. Let the chapters meet you where you are. This book is not ahead of you.

It walks beside you.

## Reflective Questions

1. Which phase of this journey feels most immediate for you right now

2. Where do you sense readiness for change, and where do you sense patience is needed

3. What would it mean to trust the order in which clarity unfolds

4. How do you typically move through transitions, with urgency or with curiosity

5. What does arrival mean to you at this stage of life

# CHAPTER 4:
# GRIEF AFTER SUCCESS,
# THE GRIEF THAT
# COMES AFTER SUCCESS

*"Grief is not a sign of weakness, nor a lack
of faith. It is the price of love."*

— Queen Elizabeth II

There is a kind of grief that does not come from loss in the traditional sense. It does not announce itself with ceremony or permission. It arrives quietly, often unexpectedly, after success. It is the grief of realization, the recognition that achieving what you worked for did not deliver everything you were promised it would.

My dearest friend Connie sat across from me, composed and articulate, describing her life with precision.

A successful career.

Adult children doing well.

Financial stability.

A calendar that finally had space in it.

She spoke calmly, almost clinically, as if outlining a case study rather than inhabiting a life.

Her smile appeared at appropriate intervals – polite,

symmetrical, steady. But it lingered a half-second too long, as if waiting for confirmation that it was the correct response.

When she mentioned how quiet the house felt now, her gaze drifted briefly toward the window. Just a flicker. When she spoke about "finally having time for herself," her fingers traced the rim of her coffee cup, circling it slowly, unconsciously.

"I worked hard for this," she said. "This is what I wanted."

And she was right.

There was no failure in her story. No visible fracture. Everything she had once aimed for had been achieved.

But as she paused between sentences, something else entered the room.

A softness around her eyes. A fatigue not of body, but of identity.

She was no longer climbing.

And she had not yet learned how to stand still.

I listened carefully, nodding, asking gentle questions. But somewhere in the middle of her words, a quiet realization moved through me.

I recognized the landscape she was describing.

Not because our lives were identical.

But because the tone was familiar.

The careful framing.

The gratitude stated clearly.

The absence of complaint.

And beneath it – a subtle disorientation.

In Connie, I saw something I had not yet admitted in myself.

The grief that follows accomplishment.

Not grief over what was lost externally, but grief over a role that no longer defines you.

For decades, our identities had been reinforced by movement, by being needed, by being decisive, by being central to action. Success had been directional. It pointed forward.

But what happens when the direction changes?

What happens when the structure that organized your energy dissolves?

As Connie spoke, I felt a small tightening in my chest, not alarm, but recognition.

I had been calling my experience fatigue.

But perhaps it was something else.

Perhaps it was the subtle grief of transition. The grief of outgrowing the very framework that once validated me. The grief of standing in spaciousness without yet knowing who I was inside it.

Watching Connie allowed me to see it without defense.

It was easier to name it in her first.

And once named, it could no longer remain hidden in me.

Grief after success does not shout. It whispers.

It shows up in polite smiles. In well-managed narratives. In sentences that begin with "I should feel..."

It does not negate pride.

It coexists with it.

And that afternoon, sitting across from my friend, I understood something with clarity:

We were not ungrateful.

We were in transition.

Some forms of grief do not come from death, divorce, or catastrophe. They arrive quietly, without ceremony or permission. It appears quietly, often unexpectedly, after success. It is the grief of realization, the recognition that achieving what you worked for did not deliver everything you were promised it would.

This grief often surprises the woman who feels it. From the outside, nothing appears wrong. Life is intact. The résumé is full. The family story has continuity. The structures that once felt stabilizing are still in place. And yet internally, something feels hollowed. A quiet ache settles in, not sharp enough to name as pain, but steady enough that it can no longer be ignored.

This is grief without permission.

Because it does not fit familiar narratives of loss, it is rarely acknowledged. There is no cultural script for grieving success. As a result, many women feel confused by their emotions. Sadness or restlessness appears at a moment that should feel satisfying. Instead of curiosity, self-judgment often follows. A woman may wonder what is wrong with her, why gratitude does not come easily, why achievement feels heavier than expected.

This misinterpretation compounds grief.

Success is not neutral. It closes doors as well as opening them. It clarifies what will no longer be possible. It brings finality to certain versions of self that were carried quietly for years as potential. When success settles into permanence, the fantasy that there will be time later dissolves.

Grief emerges not because life is wrong, but because it is real.

There is grief for the selves that were postponed. The artist who waited. The explorer who unpacked her suitcase and chose predictability. The version of womanhood deferred in the name of responsibility, stability, caregiving, or approval. These selves were not imaginary. They lived internally, shaping desire, imagination, and longing. When the path forward narrows, their absence becomes palpable.

There is also grief for the effort expended.

Many women reach success carrying exhaustion that was deferred rather than felt. During years of striving, endurance becomes a strategy. The body and psyche cooperate by postponing sensation in service of momentum. When striving slows or stops, what was held at bay begins to surface. Fatigue, sadness, or numbness may appear without a clear cause. This is not regression. It is reckoning.

Another layer of grief arises from disillusionment.

Cultural narratives promise fulfillment through

achievement, security through productivity, and meaning through contribution. These promises are not entirely false, but they are incomplete. When success delivers structure but not wholeness, women are left to reconcile the gap between expectation and lived reality. This gap is not failure. It is clarity.

Grief after success often includes mourning the simplicity of earlier striving. When goals were clear, life felt directional. Energy had somewhere to go. In the second half of life, ambiguity increases. There may be more freedom, but also less structure. The absence of obvious next steps can feel like loss, even when it is possibility in disguise.

This grief often coexists with pride.

A woman can be grateful for what she has built and still mourn what was left behind. She can love her life and still feel constrained by it. These emotions do not cancel each other out. They reflect the complexity of a life fully lived. Holding both requires emotional maturity, not resolution.

Many women attempt to bypass this grief by reinventing quickly. New projects. New goals. New forms of productivity. While reinvention can be meaningful, when it is used to avoid grief, it often recreates the same patterns that led to depletion. Grief does not respond to distraction. It asks for acknowledgment.

## When Men Reach the Same Threshold

This grief is not exclusive to women.

Men also experience grief after success, though it often arrives differently and is recognized later. For many men, identity has been closely tied to usefulness, provision, authority, or momentum. Success can reinforce these structures for decades, delaying the reckoning rather than resolving it.

When grief does arrive, it often appears behaviorally before it becomes emotional.

A man may feel it when retirement strips away daily

relevance. When health changes interrupt momentum. When authority softens and the room no longer orients itself around him. He may feel restless, irritable, or unmoored without understanding why. The language of grief may not be available to him, but the experience is no less real.

Men often grieve the loss of structure before they grieve the loss of self.

Men often grieve the loss of clear metrics, schedules, or roles that once organized their days. When those external anchors disappear, something quieter begins to surface. Without the structure that once defined their value, an internal question emerges, often unspoken: *Who am I when I am no longer needed in the same way?* They may grieve the loss of structure before they grieve the loss of self.

Where women frequently feel grief internally and relationally, men often encounter it through disruption, withdrawal, or overextension. New ventures may appear. Compulsive productivity may intensify. Or the body may intervene through illness or exhaustion, forcing a pause that language had not yet allowed.

This is not avoidance. It is socialization.

Men are often taught to move through grief by doing rather than naming. By solving rather than sitting. By rebuilding structure instead of interrogating meaning. Over time, however, the same truth surfaces. Success has a cost. Time is finite. Certain selves will not be lived.

Grief is the reckoning with that reality.

## Grief as Integration, Not Failure

Grief after success is relational for both women and men.

It can alter how partners see one another. Expectations shift. Old roles feel tighter. Conversations that once felt sufficient may now feel thin. This does not mean relationships have failed. It means the people within them have changed.

When grief is honored rather than denied, it deepens compassion. For oneself. For partners navigating their reckoning. For younger versions who did the best they could with the information they had. Grief softens judgment. It allows lives to be carried with more tenderness and less defensiveness.

This chapter does not offer a solution because grief is not a problem to solve. It is an experience to be acknowledged. In the chapters that follow, we will explore what becomes possible when grief is allowed rather than resisted. But first, it deserves to be named and respected.

If you feel this grief, you are not late. You are not broken. You are not ungrateful. You are responding honestly to a life that has unfolded with complexity and cost.

This grief is not the end of meaning.

It is often the beginning of truth.

## Reflective Questions

1. What forms of success in your life have brought unexpected sadness, restlessness, or quiet disappointment

2. Which versions of yourself do you quietly mourn, even if you rarely speak of them

3. How have cultural promises about success shaped what you expected life to feel like

4. Where do gratitude and grief coexist for you, and how do you usually respond to that tension

5. What effort, endurance, or sacrifice have you not yet allowed yourself to fully acknowledge

6. How might grief be showing up differently in the people closest to you

7. What might become possible if this grief were honored rather than avoided

# CHAPTER 5:
# RECEIVING INSTEAD
# OF ACHIEVING

*"There is a way of living that does
not require constant proving."*

— David Whyte

For many women, achievement has been the primary language of safety. It has offered structure, direction, and reassurance. Through achievement, women have learned how to secure stability, earn respect, and justify their place in the world. Achieving has not been superficial or ego driven. It has been adaptive. It has helped women navigate systems that reward output more readily than presence.

By the time a woman reaches the second half of life, achieving is often deeply ingrained. It shapes how she approaches work, relationships, health, and even her sense of self. Goals organize time. Effort defines value. Progress is measured by output and results. This orientation has carried her far. It has built lives, families, careers, and communities.

What begins to change is not competence, but appetite.

After grief is acknowledged, a subtle shift often

follows. The drive to achieve does not disappear, but it loses its dominance. Tasks feel heavier. Milestones feel less satisfying. The familiar rewards of effort no longer land in the same way. A quiet question begins to surface, sometimes without words. What if effort is no longer the primary mode of engagement? What if doing more is not the answer?

Receiving enters here, not as passivity, but as an alternative intelligence.

Receiving does not mean abandoning agency or ambition. It does not mean withdrawing from life or relinquishing responsibility. It means allowing life to offer rather than insisting it be earned. For women who have spent decades achieving, this can feel disorienting. Receiving lacks the familiar metrics of success. It cannot be tracked, optimized, or justified easily. It requires trust rather than control. It invites presence rather than performance.

Many women notice how difficult receiving actually is. Compliments are deflected. Help is declined. Pleasure is postponed. Rest is justified only after productivity. Even kindness can feel uncomfortable if it is not reciprocated quickly. This resistance is not arrogance or selfishness. It is conditioning. When worth has been tied to effort, receiving can feel undeserved or unsafe.

Receiving also exposes vulnerability.

To receive is to admit openness and interdependence. It requires letting go of the identity that says, *I am valuable because I manage, provide, endure, or carry others.* For women who have been relied upon for much of their lives, this can feel risky. Receiving asks them to soften the vigilance that once kept everything together.

My friend Sonia, described how she noticed herself turning every opportunity into a project. Invitations became obligations. Support became something to repay immediately. Even moments of ease felt provisional. When she experimented with simply accepting what was offered, without compensating for it, she felt uneasy. Over time, she also felt lighter. Receiving did not make her less capable. It softened her sense of urgency and restored her capacity to enjoy.

My sister, Zulema, noticed her resistance most clearly in her body.

She spoke about how rest never felt complete. Even when she lay down, her mind stayed alert, scanning for what should come next. Pleasure, even something as simple as a massage, felt indulgent. She felt more comfortable pushing through discomfort than allowing herself to be tended to. When her partner offered care, she would often redirect the conversation or insist she was fine.

During a period of physical exhaustion, she was forced to slow down. At first, she treated rest like a task to complete. Eventually, something shifted. She allowed herself to stay still longer than planned. She let her body receive warmth, support, touch, without explanation. The experience surprised her. What she felt was not weakness, but relief. Her body did not need to be managed. It needed to be trusted.

Receiving, she realized, was not about stopping effort. It was about loosening the grip on control. It was about ending the belief that effort was required to deserve care.

Receiving shifts the center of gravity inward.

Instead of scanning for what needs to be done next, attention moves toward what is already present. This changes how time is experienced. Moments are no longer merely transitional. They are inhabited. Life begins to feel less like a sequence of tasks and more like an unfolding experience. There is space for sensation, reflection, and meaning to register.

This does not mean effort disappears. It means effort becomes selective.

Achieving is no longer the default response to discomfort or uncertainty. Sometimes the wisest action is to pause, allow, or listen. Receiving teaches discernment. It asks whether action is truly required or whether presence is sufficient. It creates room to sense what is being asked rather than reacting out of habit.

Receiving also alters relationships.

When women stop proving their worth by staying busy, deflecting compliments, and declining help, connection becomes less transactional. Help can be accepted without guilt. Love can be received without repayment. Attention can be enjoyed without performance. This deepens intimacy and reduces exhaustion. Relationships become places of exchange rather than endurance.

Many women fear that receiving will make them complacent or dependent. In practice, the opposite often occurs. When receiving is integrated, energy replenishes. Creativity returns. Desire clarifies. Action becomes more intentional rather than compulsive. Effort begins to flow from fullness rather than depletion.

Receiving is not a technique to master. It is an orientation, a shift in how you relate to care, pleasure, and support.

It often begins in small, unremarkable ways. Allowing rest without justification. Letting a compliment land without deflection. Accepting assistance without apology. Enjoying something without earning it first. These moments may feel uncomfortable at first. That discomfort is not a signal to stop. It is a sign that a deeper pattern is loosening.

Over time, receiving becomes a form of self-respect.

It signals that a woman trusts her inherent worth. That she no longer needs to extract value from every moment. That life does not have to be conquered to be meaningful. Receiving affirms that existence itself is sufficient justification for care, pleasure, and support.

In the second half of life, receiving often becomes more natural. The body signals limits. Time feels finite. The illusion that everything must be earned begins to crack. Receiving offers a way to live with less force and more grace, without abandoning engagement or contribution.

This chapter does not argue that achieving was wrong.

It honors what achievement made possible and the resilience it required. It simply invites a new balance, one where effort and openness coexist, where contribution flows from coherence rather than compulsion. It

Receiving instead of achieving is not a retreat from life. It is a deeper participation in it.

## Reflective Questions

1. How has achievement shaped your sense of worth over time

2. Where do you notice resistance to receiving support, rest, or appreciation

3. What fears arise when you imagine not earning everything you receive

4. How does your body respond when you allow yourself to receive without justification

5. In what areas of life might receiving bring more clarity than effort

6. How do your relationships change when you stop proving your value

7. What would it mean to trust that you are worthy of what comes to you now

# CHAPTER 6:
# THE COURAGE TO BE UNNEEDED, RELEASING ROLES WITHOUT LOSING RELEVANCE

*"There is a season for usefulness, and there
is a season for presence. Both are sacred."*

— Clarissa Pinkola Estés

For much of life, being needed feels like love and proof of value. We are praised for our reliability, our availability, our willingness to step in and hold things together. Over time, usefulness becomes more than something we do. It becomes how we belong.

Eventually, roles solidify. We are known as the problem solver, the caretaker, the strong one, the dependable one. Being needed feels stabilizing. It answers the question of who we are – sometimes so completely that we stop asking anything deeper.

This shift became clear when I caught myself saying yes automatically. Yes, to helping. Yes, to stepping in. Yes, to filling gaps others had not learned to fill. Often, I was not being asked. I was anticipating. I was responding to an internal expectation that my value depended on being indispensable.

There was comfort in that pattern. There was also erosion of desire, of rest, of the quiet joy that once came easily.

One afternoon, I chose not to intervene in a situation I would normally manage.

We were seated around a conference table reviewing a proposal that had begun to wobble. The projections were slightly misaligned. The timeline felt optimistic. I could see the weak points instantly – years of experience had trained my eye to detect risk before it surfaced.

The room grew quiet.

This was the moment when I would usually lean forward and recalibrate everything. I knew the language. I knew the fix. I could have restored order in under a minute.

My body prepared to act – a small inhale, a shift in posture, the familiar gathering of words.

And then I paused.

I let the silence extend.

It felt unnatural. Almost negligent.

A part of me equated intervention with responsibility. If I saw the flaw and did not correct it, was I complicit? Was I withholding competence?

The discomfort in the room stretched.

Then someone else spoke.

Tentatively at first. Then with more clarity. The flawed assumption was named. The forecast was reconsidered. The timeline adjusted. Ownership shifted.

No one turned to me for rescue.

Nothing collapsed.

In fact, something strengthened.

As the discussion reorganized itself without my orchestration, I felt a subtle but profound shift inside me. The reflex to control had not come from ego. It had come from identity.

For decades, being capable had meant being central.

Being responsible had meant being necessary. Being empathetic had meant anticipating and smoothing what others hesitated to confront.

Control, in that context, was not domination. It was protection. It was efficiency. It was care.

But in the second half of life, the architecture of identity begins to change.

We are no longer building from scratch. We are no longer proving competence. We are no longer securing position. The urgency that once fueled control begins to soften.

What remains is a deeper question:

Who am I if I am not the one holding everything together?

Control often disguises itself as virtue. It whispers that if we loosen our grip, standards will fall, relationships will strain, outcomes will suffer.

But sometimes control is simply fear in refined clothing.

Fear of irrelevance.

Fear of being unnecessary.

Fear of watching others struggle.

The discipline of that afternoon was not silence for its own sake. It was trust.

Trust that others could rise.

Trust that leadership does not require constant assertion.

Trust that my value in the room did not depend on being indispensable.

In earlier seasons, control built stability. It created security for my family, my colleagues, my clients. It was appropriate then.

But in this season, control began to feel heavy.

The second half of life invites a different posture.

Less gripping.

More allowing.

Less orchestrating.

More witnessing.

It asks us to move from being essential to being expansive. From managing outcomes to mentoring capacity. From directing energy outward to rediscovering it within.

Letting go of control is not passivity. It is maturation.

It is trusting that the systems we helped build can function without constant supervision. It is trusting that the people we invested in can navigate complexity without our immediate correction. It is trusting that identity is not erased when activity decreases.

The most surprising realization was this:

When I loosened my grip, I did not disappear.

I became lighter.

And in that lightness, something new began to form – not based on being needed, but on being aligned.

That was when I understood that releasing roles is not the same as losing relevance. Relevance rooted in obligation is fragile; it requires constant reinforcement. But relevance rooted in presence endures. It does not depend on demand. It rests in being rather than doing.

The courage to be unneeded is not withdrawal. It is trust.

I have seen this shift most poignantly in families, particularly between parents and adult children. My friend Joan struggled deeply with stepping back from her grown children's lives. She believed that love meant constant availability, advice, and protection. She feared that if she stopped offering solutions, she would become invisible.

When she finally chose restraint – not indifference, but respect – her relationships changed. Her children did not drift away. They leaned in differently. Conversations became more thoughtful. Requests became more intentional. Advice, when offered, carried more weight because it was no longer constant. Being unneeded created space for mutuality rather than dependence.

In partnerships, this shift can be transformative.

When roles soften, connection deepens. No one is cast as the rescuer or the dependent. No one carries the emotional labor alone. Two adults meet instead of two functions. Love no longer flows through obligation, but through choice.

One man shared that when he stopped being the fixer in his marriage, always managing emotions, logistics, and outcomes, his wife stepped into her authority. Their relationship became lighter. Desire returned. Respect grew. Letting go of the role did not weaken the bond. It strengthened it.

There is also a profound internal shift when roles dissolve.

Energy once spent maintaining usefulness becomes available for curiosity, creativity, and rest. Questions emerge that were previously postponed. What do I enjoy when no one is watching? What draws me when there is no outcome attached? What feels true rather than necessary?

This season invites a different form of contribution.

Instead of doing more, you transmit more calm, perspective, steadiness, and wisdom. These qualities cannot be forced or scheduled. They are sensed. They arrive through presence rather than effort.

I have noticed that people gravitate toward those who are no longer hustling for relevance. There is something grounding about someone who is at ease with not being necessary. Their presence feels settled. Their words carry weight because they are not competing for attention. Their silence is not empty. It is spacious.

Releasing roles also requires grieving.

You may mourn identities that once defined you: the leader, the caregiver, the achiever. Letting go does not erase the years those roles mattered. It honors them by allowing evolution. Grief here is not regret. It is respect for what was carried faithfully and is now ready to be set down.

You are not becoming less. You are becoming freer.

To live without being needed is to discover that your

worth was never conditional. You do not have to earn belonging through usefulness. You belong because you are here, because your presence matters independently of function.

In this truth, relevance becomes quieter, deeper, and far more lasting. It no longer demands performance. It does not fade when roles change. It endures because it is rooted in being rather than necessity.

## Reflective Questions

1. Which roles have most strongly shaped your sense of value throughout your life?

2. Where do you continue to be needed out of habit rather than true necessity?

3. What emotions arise when you imagine stepping back from certain roles – relief, fear, grief, freedom?

4. In what ways might your presence be more valuable than your intervention?

5. What new forms of contribution could emerge if you allowed yourself to be unneeded?

# CHAPTER 7:
# FRIENDSHIP IN THE SECOND HALF OF LIFE

*"Some people walk with us for a season.*
*Some for a lifetime. Wisdom is knowing the difference.*

— Maria L. Ellis

Friendship changes in the second half of life, often more quietly than any other relationship. There is rarely a clear ending — no defining conversation, no dramatic rupture. Instead, there is a gradual shift that is easy to overlook at first. Calls are returned more slowly. Invitations are postponed rather than declined. Conversations feel shallower, more polite, less revealing. The effort required to stay connected increases while the nourishment subtly decreases. Many women sense this long before they are willing to name it.

Because friendship is chosen rather than assigned, its evolution can feel especially disorienting.

When marriages shift, there is language for it. When careers end or transition, there are ceremonies, retirement dinners, LinkedIn announcements, farewell speeches. Structure exists. Social permission exists.

But when a friendship loosens, there is rarely a script.

I think of my friend Diane.

We met during the years when life was full and fast. Children still at home. Careers ascending. Calendars tight. We bonded over logistics at first – carpools, school events, shared frustration over late meetings and early practices. What began as convenience deepened into affection.

Diane was quick-witted, decisive, fiercely loyal. She had a laugh that arrived before the punchline fully formed. We walked neighborhoods together in the evenings, solving the world in brisk strides. We compared notes on parenting, business, aging parents. We were, in many ways, aligned.

For years, our rhythm was steady.

But seasons change quietly.

As my interior life began shifting – less urgency, more reflection – our conversations began to feel slightly out of sync. She remained energized by expansion: new committees, new initiatives, new social circles. I found myself craving depth over motion.

One afternoon over lunch, she leaned forward, animated.

"You need to get involved in this," she insisted. "You'd be perfect for it. They need someone strong."

I smiled. A familiar description. Someone strong.

"I'm not sure I want to be needed like that right now," I said gently.

She paused, just briefly.

"What do you mean?" she asked.

I searched for language that did not sound like rejection.

"I think I'm in a different season," I replied. "Less building. More... listening."

She nodded politely. But the current shifted.

It was not a dramatic fracture. There was no betrayal. No harsh words. Just a gradual thinning of shared momentum.

Calls became less frequent. Invitations were declined more often, not out of anger, but out of honesty. The long walks shortened. Then stopped.

And here is the awkward truth no one teaches you:

There is no formal ending to a friendship that simply evolves.

You do not schedule a closing conversation.

You do not draft a statement.

You do not return the final call with, "I no longer align with this version of us."

Instead, you hesitate.

You let one call go to voicemail because you do not have the energy for the familiar cadence. You tell yourself you will return it later. Later stretches. The text thread grows quiet.

And then comes the uncomfortable self-interrogation:

*Am I being selfish?*

*Have I become distant?*

*Is this avoidance or discernment?*

Because women are taught that loyalty is a virtue, and distance implies fault.

For a while, I assumed the shift must be my failing; that perhaps I had grown less generous, less available, less interesting.

But eventually, I understood something quieter.

Friendship, like identity, is seasonal.

Diane had not done anything wrong. Nor had I.

We had simply grown in different directions.

She continued to build outward. I began building inward.

The loss was not explosive. It was subtle. And that subtlety made it harder to honor. There was no socially sanctioned grief for friendships that fade without conflict.

Yet I felt it.

Not as anger.

Not as resentment.

But as tenderness for what we had shared.

The truth is, when friendships loosen, what we often grieve is not the person alone. We grieve the version of ourselves who existed most fully in that dynamic.

With Diane, I was the ambitious, solution-oriented woman in constant motion. As I softened, that version softened too.

And when I stopped returning calls immediately, what I was really doing was pausing long enough to ask:

Does this still feel like truth?

The second half of life requires discernment that can appear, from the outside, like withdrawal.

But discernment is not cruelty.

It is alignment.

And sometimes, loving someone includes allowing the relationship to take a different shape, even if that shape is distance.

When partnerships change, there is language for it. When careers end or shift, there is structure and social permission. When friendships loosen, women often assume the cause must be personal. Loyalty is questioned. They wonder if they have become difficult, selfish, or emotionally unavailable. They search for fault rather than meaning.

In reality, friendship is deeply shaped by who we are becoming.

Earlier in life, many friendships are formed through proximity and shared necessity. Children, work, caregiving, neighborhoods, and mutual striving create powerful bonds. These friendships are real and often lifesaving. They carry women through seasons of exhaustion, growth, and survival. They provide companionship during years when energy is directed outward and identity is closely tied to responsibility.

But these friendships are often built around who a woman needed to be at that time: the competent one, the accommodating one, the listener, the organizer, the one who shows up no matter what. As life changes, those identities may loosen. When they do, the friendships shaped by them may loosen as well.

As identity shifts in the second half of life, relational

needs change. Performance gives way to presence. Validation gives way to truth. Many women find they no longer want friendships that require constant explanation, emotional management, or self-editing. They notice a new sensitivity to tone, depth, and reciprocity. What once felt familiar now feels effortful. What once felt supportive now feels misaligned.

This realization often brings grief.

Women grieve friendships that did not end badly – friendships that simply no longer fit. They grieve shared history and shared shorthand. They grieve the comfort of being known through time, of having someone who remembers earlier versions of themselves. They grieve the fantasy that certain friendships would remain unchanged forever, untouched by growth or difference.

This grief is complicated by a lack of permission. Few women feel allowed to mourn friendships that fade without conflict. There is no clear reason to point to, no wrongdoing to explain the loss. The ending feels illegitimate. And yet the absence is deeply felt.

One woman described noticing that she left lunches with a longtime friend feeling drained rather than connected. Nothing was overtly wrong. The conversations were polite and even affectionate. They laughed. They exchanged updates. And yet she felt unseen, as if the deeper parts of her were no longer welcome at the table. When she finally admitted this to herself, she felt both sadness and relief. The friendship had been anchored in who she used to be, not who she was becoming.

Another woman shared that after retiring, she realized how many friendships had been structured around complaint and commiseration. Work had provided a shared language of frustration and endurance. When that context disappeared, the connections dissolved. At first, she felt abandoned and confused. Over time, she recognized that those friendships had completed their purpose. They had served her faithfully in one season and were not meant to follow her into the next.

Friendship in the second half of life becomes more selective, not because women are less generous, but because energy is no longer limitless. Time is felt more acutely. Emotional labor carries a clearer cost. Women ask, often without conscious intention, "Where do I feel most like myself? Where do I feel relaxed rather than vigilant? Where do I feel seen without having to explain?"

This clarity often creates a season of in-between.

Old friendships fall away. New ones have not yet formed. The social world may feel quieter. Invitations are fewer. The calendar opens. Many women interpret this as loneliness or failure, when it is often a transitional space. A clearing. A pause between versions of connection. This space can feel uncomfortable, especially for women who are accustomed to being socially anchored. Yet it is often necessary for new forms of friendship to emerge.

New friendships in this stage tend to form differently. They are less rooted in shared struggle and more in shared presence. Less about loyalty to history and more about resonance in the present. These friendships often feel lighter, even when they are deep. Silence is easier. Difference is less threatening. There is less need to impress, accommodate, or perform.

One woman described meeting a friend in her sixties with whom she could speak openly from the beginning. There was no backstory to maintain and no identity to protect. The friendship felt immediate, not because it was intense, but because it was honest. Each woman met the other as she was, without expectation or role.

Another woman noticed that her most satisfying connections were no longer one-size-fits-all. She had different friends for different dimensions of her life. A walking friend who shared her love of movement and quiet conversation. A creative friend with whom ideas flowed easily. A spiritual friend who could sit with questions rather than answers. Releasing the expectation that one person meets all needs brought unexpected relief and freedom.

Friendship in the second half of life is not about consolidation.

It is about alignment.

Letting friendships change does not require cutting people off or burning bridges. It requires releasing expectations. Some friendships become seasonal. Some remain warm but infrequent. Some soften into memory. Others reemerge later in new forms. Allowing relationships to settle where they naturally belong creates less resentment and more truth.

This chapter is not an argument for withdrawal. It is an invitation to notice where friendship nourishes and where it depletes. To allow grief without judgment. To trust that friendships can change shape without something having gone wrong.

You are not failing at friendship if your circle changes. You are responding honestly to who you are becoming.

Some friendships will remain anchors.

Others will become memories.

Still others will surprise you.

All of this belongs to a life lived with integrity.

## Reflective Questions

1. How have your friendships changed over the past decade?

2. Which relationships feel nourishing, and which feel effortful?

3. Where do you notice yourself maintaining connection out of history rather than resonance?

4. What grief arises when friendships fade without conflict?

5. How do you experience periods of relational in-between?

6.   What kinds of friendship feel most aligned with who you are now?

7.   Where might releasing expectation bring more honesty and ease?

8.   How would your friendships change if self-blame were removed from the equation?

# CHAPTER 8:
# VISIBILITY WITHOUT PERFORMANCE, BEING SEEN WITHOUT PROVING

*"To be seen without striving is a form of freedom."*

— David Whyte

My farewell as President of the Empire State NYC Branch of AAUW did not take place in a ballroom.

It unfolded in small rectangles on a screen.

It was a Zoom gathering, and many AAUW New York State leaders were present. Familiar faces appeared in tidy digital frames: home offices, bookshelves, carefully positioned lamps. The chat window filled steadily:

*Congratulations!*

*Thank you for your leadership!*

*So grateful for your service!*

Even digitally, I knew how to occupy the role.

I had prepared a structured reflection: accomplishments, membership growth, initiatives completed, scholarships funded, strategic partnerships strengthened. The narrative was strong. We had done meaningful work.

I unmuted myself.

The gallery view reflected back at me, dozens of women who had watched me lead through complexity. Women who had seen me facilitate meetings, negotiate tension, hold firm when needed.

For years, I had been visible because I performed leadership well.

I began as expected: gratitude, acknowledgment, and measurable outcomes. My voice was steady. Clear. Competent.

And then I looked at my small square in the corner of the screen.

There I was: composed, articulate, and presidential.

Suddenly, the performance felt almost too familiar.

I paused.

The silence felt longer on Zoom than it ever would in a room. In digital space, silence can feel like malfunction. I could see a few faces shift slightly, wondering if my audio had cut out.

But I stayed.

"I want to name something we don't usually put in our reports," I said.

The chat stopped scrolling.

"There is a moment that comes after you've done the job well, after you've given your energy, your structure, your steadiness. It's the moment when the title begins to loosen."

I felt my chest tighten slightly as I continued.

"For many years, I have been the steady one in this role. The one you could count on. And while I am deeply proud of what we've built together, I would be dishonest if I didn't admit that leadership carries a quiet loneliness."

There it was.

Unscripted. Unpolished.

I spoke about the fatigue that does not show up in board minutes. About the subtle grief that follows completion. About what I now call *The Disorientation of Arrival*, the moment when you reach what you worked toward and realize that identity must now reorganize.

Faces softened.

Some women leaned closer to their screens. Others remained still, listening.

When I finished, the response was different than usual.

The applause icon flashed. Hearts floated up briefly. The chat resumed, but slower.

Afterward, several private messages arrived.

"Thank you for saying that."

"I've felt this too but never had language for it."

"I thought it was just me."

But there were also quieter signals.

One leader said, kindly but carefully, "You've always been so strong. It's strange to hear you talk about loneliness."

Strange.

When visibility has been built on performance, authenticity can feel destabilizing.

In the weeks that followed, I noticed subtle changes. Fewer immediate requests to step into high-profile roles. Less assumption that I would naturally chair the next initiative. The title "President" disappeared from email signatures almost overnight.

No confrontation. No conflict.

Just recalibration.

For years, I had been visible because I carried responsibility visibly.

Now I was visible because I spoke truth.

And those two forms of visibility are not received the same way.

That Zoom farewell marked the beginning of something I now call Presence-Based Visibility.

Visibility that does not depend on performance.

Visibility that does not rise or fall with titles.

Visibility that exists because you are inhabiting yourself fully, not because you are managing outcomes.

It cost something tangible.

Influence shifted. Invitations thinned. The urgency of being needed softened.

But what it returned was deeper freedom.

The freedom to be seen without striving.

The freedom to occupy space without proving.

The freedom to exist without amplifying myself to meet expectation.

In the second half of life, that freedom becomes essential.

Because performance sustains status.

Presence sustains identity.

And identity, once untethered from applause, even digital applause, becomes steady in a different way.

When the final well-wishes were shared and the meeting formally adjourned, the screen began to empty.

One by one, the rectangles disappeared.

*Leave Meeting.*

The gallery view collapsed into a single square, my face reflected back at me in the darkened screen.

The room around me was quiet. No applause echoing. No cluster of women gathering afterward. No lingering embrace.

Just the faint hum of my laptop.

I closed it slowly.

And in the silence that followed, I felt something I had not anticipated.

Sadness.

Not dramatic. Not overwhelming. But unmistakable.

A hollowing.

For many years, I had carried that role. I had advocated for pay equity. I had supported educational initiatives for women and girls. I had chaired difficult conversations, navigated state-level dynamics, held steady through transitions. For over twenty-five years, my life had been woven into the advancement of women in boardrooms, in classrooms, in policy discussions.

And now the title was gone.

The calls slowed. The urgency dissipated.

I felt, if I am honest, unappreciated.

Not because no one thanked me. They had.

But because once the role concluded, the need concluded with it.

There is a particular vulnerability in realizing that some forms of visibility are tied to function.

When the function ends, the spotlight moves.

Sitting there, I allowed myself to feel it fully.

The disappointment.

The ego bruise.

The quiet question: *Did it matter?*

And then something steadier surfaced.

Of course it mattered.

But it was never about me.

The mission had never been personal elevation. It was pay equity for women. It was scholarships for girls. It was leadership pathways for those coming next. It was ensuring that doors remained open wider than we found them.

The work was not designed to center me.

It was designed to outlast me.

That realization did not erase the sadness immediately. But it reframed it.

I had mistaken visibility for validation.

What I truly cared about was impact.

Impact does not always applaud you at the end.

Sometimes it simply continues.

The mission of advancing women does not need a president's title to move forward. It needs collective commitment. It needs continuity.

And if my season of visible leadership had ended, that did not mean my value had ended.

It meant the baton had passed.

In that quiet room, with my laptop closed and the glow of the screen fading, I understood something essential:

Presence without performance means serving without centering yourself.

It means allowing your work to speak without insisting that you remain the voice delivering it.

It means trusting that what you built can stand without your constant visibility.

The sadness softened.

What remained was clarity.

My worth was never meant to be tethered to a role.

And the mission, the education of women and girls, the pursuit of equity, had never been about recognition.

It was about progress.

The second half of life asks us to serve without attachment to spotlight.

To contribute without anchoring identity to applause.

To be seen, yes, but not to depend on being needed.

That night, after the Zoom window closed and the title dissolved, I stepped quietly into a different form of leadership.

One not based on performance.

One based on presence.

For much of life, visibility is earned. We are seen because we achieve, perform, contribute, or carry responsibility. Attention arrives as a response to usefulness. Approval follows effort. Worth is often confused with output. Being visible means being impressive, reliable, or necessary.

This orientation is not accidental. It is reinforced early and often. We learn that recognition comes when we do more, manage better, or hold things together. Visibility becomes transactional. If we contribute enough, we are noticed. If we perform well, we are affirmed. Over time, this logic becomes internalized. We no longer question it.

Then, quietly, a new question arises.

Who am I when I no longer prove anything?

At first, this question can feel unsettling. Performance has structure. It gives shape to identity. It offers cues about how to behave and what is expected. Without it, many fear invisibility. They worry that if they stop striving, they will disappear. That without effort, there will be no acknowledgment, no place, no relevance.

Yet in the later seasons of life, something profound becomes possible. The ability to be seen without performing.

I first noticed this shift when I spoke less in rooms where I once led conversations. Not because I had less to say, but because I no longer needed to demonstrate insight. I listened more carefully. I allowed pauses. And unexpectedly, people leaned in. When I did speak, my words landed differently. My presence carried weight not through assertion, but through steadiness.

This is the paradox of mature visibility.

When performance falls away, authenticity becomes visible.

A woman I know spent decades as the emotional anchor of her family. She mediated conflicts, anticipated needs, and regulated the emotional climate wherever she went. Her value was unquestioned, but it was conditional. When she finally stopped managing every interaction, she feared being dismissed or overlooked. Instead, something else happened. Some people pulled away. Others came closer. Those who remained were drawn not to her caretaking, but to her clarity. She was no longer performing connection. She was inhabiting it.

Visibility without performance is not passive.

It is rooted.

It arises from coherence rather than effort. In earlier years, being seen often meant being impressive. In this season, it means being real. The shift is subtle but profound. Instead of asking, "How am I being perceived?" the question becomes, "Am I aligned with myself?"

This shift often becomes visible after major transitions.

One man shared that after retiring, he felt invisible for the first time. Without a title or authority, he felt unmoored. At first, he compensated by talking more. He referenced past accomplishments. He explained who he had been.

Eventually, he stopped. He allowed himself to arrive without credentials. The need to prove himself began to ease. People responded not to his history, but to his presence. He was seen not for what he had done, but for who he was becoming.

This kind of visibility cannot be manufactured.

It emerges when self-respect replaces self-promotion. When a person no longer needs to announce themselves, their presence speaks quietly and clearly. This visibility is not loud. It does not demand attention. It is sensed.

Being seen without proving also reshapes intimacy.

Relationships become less transactional. You are no longer valued for what you provide, but for who you are. This can be disorienting at first. Without performance, the familiar scripts fall away. You may notice which relationships were sustained by effort rather than mutual presence. You may also notice which ones deepen when explanation is no longer required.

I noticed that when I stopped over-explaining my choices, I felt more visible, not less. Silence carried confidence. Boundaries communicated self-trust. Presence replaced justification. I did not need to persuade others to understand me. I trusted that alignment would speak for itself.

Not everyone responds well to this shift.

Those accustomed to your performance may resist your authenticity. They may misinterpret your steadiness as withdrawal or indifference. They may attempt to re-engage you through old expectations. This is not a failure. It is information. It reveals which connections were anchored in role rather than relationship.

Visibility without performance is not about disappearing.

It is about integrity.

You are still engaged. You are still expressive. You are still contributing. But now, you do so from choice rather than obligation. You speak when it matters. You show up without needing to manage perception. You allow yourself to be seen as you are, not as you were expected to be.

In this season of life, being seen is no longer the goal.

It is a byproduct of alignment.

And perhaps the most powerful visibility of all is this: Knowing when you are acting from truth rather than habit. Feeling at home in your presence. Trusting that you do not need to prove your worth in order to be real.

This is not invisibility.

It is freedom.

## Reflective Questions

1. Where in your life do you still perform in order to be valued?

2. How do you feel when you imagine being seen without explaining or proving yourself?

3. Which relationships depend on your performance, and which honor your presence?

4. What changes when you prioritize self-alignment over external validation?

5. How might your life feel if visibility were rooted in authenticity rather than effort?

# CHAPTER 9:
# LOVE WITHOUT
# OBLIGATION

*"Love does not begin where obligation ends,
it is revealed there."*

— Esther Perel

For much of life, love is closely intertwined with responsibility. We show up because we are needed. We stay involved because it would be disappointing not to. We offer care, attention, and effort not always from desire, but from duty. Love becomes something we maintain.

This is not wrong. It is human. Families, partnerships, and communities depend on reliability. But over time, obligation can quietly replace choice. Love becomes predictable, functional, and sometimes heavy. It is measured by effort rather than presence.

In the later seasons of life, a different question begins to surface.

What remains of love when obligation is no longer doing the work?

For many, this question arises first in family settings, gatherings layered with history, roles, and unspoken expectations. Holidays have a way of revealing who we are expected to be.

I had always been the emotional stabilizer at family gatherings. I remembered birthdays. Smoothed tensions. Redirected difficult conversations. If someone felt overlooked or misunderstood, I noticed. If silence grew uncomfortable, I filled it. My presence kept things pleasant, manageable, intact.

One Thanksgiving, I decided to do something unfamiliar.

I arrived with no agenda to manage the room.

The house was loud when I walked in, dishes clattering, overlapping conversations, children running through the hallway. In previous years, I would have immediately begun scanning for undercurrents: Who looks tense? Who needs help? Who might clash? This time, I took off my coat slowly. I sat down before offering help. I listened.

At the table, a familiar dynamic emerged. A comment was made, slightly sharp, slightly dismissive. Normally, I would have softened it with humor or changed the subject. Instead, I stayed quiet. The silence stretched longer than usual. Someone shifted in their chair. Another person cleared their throat.

Then something unexpected happened.

Someone else spoke up. Not to smooth things over, but to respond honestly. The conversation stumbled, then steadied. It was imperfect, a little awkward, but real. No one looked at me to rescue the moment.

Later, as dessert was served, a family member sat beside me and said, "You seem different today." I smiled and replied, "I'm just here." That was the moment I realized what had changed. I had not withdrawn from the family. I had withdrawn from obligation.

After that dinner, I began noticing something else.

My sons, strong, capable, married, building lives of their own, still looked to me in familiar ways. Not for survival. Not for authority. But for continuity.

"Mom, can you handle that?"

"Mom, what do you think we should do?"

"Mom, can you just coordinate it?"

The requests were not unreasonable. In many cases, they were practical. For years, I had been the organizer, the memory-keeper, the stabilizer. I knew birthdays, preferences, logistics, medical histories, holiday traditions. I could hold ten threads in my head without effort.

And part of me loved being needed.

That is the part we rarely admit.

Being needed affirms relevance.

But the second half of life introduces a necessary recalibration.

If we continue carrying responsibility long after it is required, we quietly deny our children the dignity of leadership in their lives.

The difficulty is not logistical.

It is emotional.

When you stop automatically coordinating, your grown children may interpret it as withdrawal.

When you say, "I trust you to decide," they may hear distance instead of empowerment.

When you decline to manage details, they may feel momentarily unsupported.

And you will feel the pull.

The old reflex will rise quickly:

- It's easier if I just do it.

- Why create friction?

- They're busy; I have more time.

But growth requires discomfort on both sides.

At one point, I gently said to one of my sons, "You're capable of handling this. I trust your judgment."

There was a pause.

"Of course I can," he replied, slightly defensive. "I just thought you'd want to."

That sentence revealed the core dynamic.

For years, wanting and being responsible had been intertwined.

I had to untangle them.

"I do want to be involved," I clarified. "But I don't need to run it."

That distinction matters.

Not running something does not mean not caring.

It means redefining contribution.

Dealing with family expectations in this season requires three internal shifts:

1.  Separate love from labor.

2.  You can love deeply without managing constantly.

3.  Allow your sons to feel the weight of their adulthood.

4.  Responsibility strengthens when it is carried, not when it is cushioned.

5.  Accept that their discomfort – and yours – is temporary.

6.  The first few times you step back will feel awkward. That awkwardness is growth in motion.

There may be moments when they misinterpret your restraint. There may be moments when you question yourself. That is natural.

But remember this:

You are not relinquishing motherhood.

You are evolving it.

In the first half of life, motherhood is

directive, protective, coordinating. In the second half, it becomes advisory, supportive, observational.

You move from being the engine to being the compass.

Your grown children do not need you to disappear.

They need you to shift.

And if you do it with clarity – not resentment, not withdrawal, but grounded presence – they will eventually rise into the space you leave open.

The goal is not to be unnecessary.

The goal is to be freely chosen.

That is a different kind of bond.

And a stronger one.

In doing so, I became more present, not less. My attention was no longer split between managing everyone else and inhabiting myself. Love was no longer rooted in vigilance. It flowed through choice.

This is how love reorganizes when obligation loosens. Some relationships deepen. Others recalibrate. A few may fade. When love is no longer maintained through effort alone, it reveals which connections are sustained by mutual presence rather than dependence.

Another person described this shift differently. For years, he had been the one who absorbed emotional tension in his family. If someone was upset, he listened. If conflict arose, he mediated. He believed love meant endurance. When he finally stopped absorbing what was not his to carry, the family dynamic changed. Conversations became shorter. But when connection happened, it was clearer. Less burdened. More honest.

Love without obligation is not detached. It is discerning. It asks: *Am I here because I choose to be, or because I feel responsible for holding everything together?* The difference is subtle, but transformative.

In partnerships, this shift can feel both liberating and unsettling. When love is no longer expressed through constant accommodation, patterns are exposed. Some partners discover a deeper intimacy – one based on desire rather than duty. Others must renegotiate how they relate without familiar scripts.

This is not a loss of love. It is a refinement.

When obligation recedes, love becomes visible in new ways, in effortless laughter, in shared silence, in the steady assurance that boundaries do not end belonging.

I have noticed that when obligation fades, love grows quieter but stronger. It no longer announces itself through sacrifice. It shows up through presence. Through honesty. Through the willingness to remain without managing outcomes.

Love without obligation does not mean love without care. It means love without compulsion.

It means choosing connection rather than performing it. Allowing relationships to breathe. Trusting that what is real will remain when effort is no longer propping it up.

In this season of life, love is no longer proven by how much you do. It is revealed by how fully you are willing to be present and how freely you allow others to do the same.

This is not less love. It is truer love.

## Reflective Questions

1. Where in your relationships does obligation still substitute for choice?

2. In what situations do you feel responsible for maintaining harmony or connection?

3. What might change if you allowed others to carry their emotional weight?

4. Which relationships deepen when effort decreases – and which rely on obligation to survive?

5. How would love feel if it were expressed through presence rather than responsibility?

# CHAPTER 10:
# INTIMACY AND DESIRE, RECLAIMING ALIVENESS THROUGH AUTHENTIC CONNECTION

*"Desire thrives in safety, not in performance."*

— Esther Perel

For many women, desire fades quietly. Not because it has disappeared, but because the conditions that once supported it no longer exist. Desire is often misunderstood as something that diminishes inevitably with age, time, or changing bodies. In truth, desire recedes most often when a woman no longer feels safe to be herself. When intimacy becomes performative, desire withdraws.

Performance in intimacy is subtle. It does not always look like pretending or deception. More often, it looks like accommodation. Anticipation. Emotional management. A woman learns to read the room, sense her partner's needs, and adjust herself accordingly. She becomes skilled at minimizing disruption and keeping connection intact. Over time, intimacy becomes something she provides rather than something she inhabits.

Desire does not disappear in this process.

It goes underground.

Many women interpret fading desire as a personal failing. They assume something is wrong with their bodies or their capacity for connection. They try to fix themselves through effort, education, or endurance. They push past discomfort and override reluctance. These attempts rarely restore desire. They often deepen the disconnection.

Desire is not sustained by effort.

It is sustained by safety.

Safety in intimacy is not merely predictability or routine. It is emotional truth. A woman feels safe when she does not have to manage her partner's reactions, protect the relationship from honesty, or suppress parts of herself to maintain connection. When she can say no without punishment, express need without apology, and change without fear of abandonment, her body softens. Desire begins to stir.

Without this safety, the body contracts. Desire retreats.

One woman described how she believed her loss of desire was something she needed to correct. She read books, tried harder, and pushed herself past discomfort. Nothing changed. Only when she stopped performing did something shift. She began speaking more honestly. She set clearer boundaries. She allowed herself to disappoint rather than disappear.

Authentic intimacy requires mutual presence.

It cannot survive where one person is consistently self-monitoring. Desire emerges when a woman feels free to respond rather than comply. When her yes is fully chosen and her no is respected, her nervous system relaxes. Aliveness returns. Desire becomes less risky when it is not demanded or evaluated.

Desire also requires permission.

Many women internalize the belief that desire is indulgent, disruptive, or inappropriate in the second half of life. Cultural narratives often render women less visible, less expressive, and less alive as they age. These messages do not extinguish desire. They teach women to withhold it. Over time, withholding becomes habit. Desire is postponed, minimized, or redirected into productivity and caretaking.

Eventually, a woman may lose touch with what desire feels like in her body.

This is not loss.

It is dormancy.

Reclaiming desire does not begin with action. It begins with honesty. What feels constraining? Where am I performing? What parts of myself have I muted to preserve connection? These questions are not about blame. They are about clarity. They allow a woman to notice the conditions under which desire has learned to hide.

Intimacy without authenticity is exhausting.

Intimacy with authenticity is restoring.

The difference is not technique. It is truth. When a woman allows herself to be seen as she is, rather than as she should be, desire becomes possible again. This does not require perfection or constant closeness. It requires reality. Desire can survive tension when honesty is present. It fades quietly when silence replaces truth.

One woman described how her relationship changed when she stopped prioritizing peace over honesty. At first, conversations were uncomfortable. Desire felt distant. There was uncertainty and awkwardness. Over time, something unexpected happened. She felt more present in her body. She laughed more easily. Desire returned not as urgency or pressure, but as warmth and curiosity. It felt sustainable rather than something she had to perform.

Desire is not urgency.

It is aliveness.

It does not demand constant expression or validation. It asks for permission to exist. When a woman no longer apologizes for her wants or suppresses her no, desire feels less dangerous. It becomes integrated rather than explosive. It no longer needs to hide or rush.

This chapter is not an argument for constant intimacy or heightened sexuality. It is an argument for alignment. Desire reflects the state of connection – not only with a partner, but with oneself. It mirrors how honestly a woman inhabits her body, her truth, her longing.

When she says yes out of obligation while her body tightens, desire quiets.

When she agrees to closeness while resentment lingers unspoken, desire withdraws.

When she softens into what she genuinely wants, whether that is touch, space, laughter, or stillness, desire responds.

Alignment is not about intensity. It is about congruence. It is the absence of internal negotiation. When connection is authentic, desire returns as warmth and curiosity.

When connection is managed, it retreats.

As women age, desire often becomes more nuanced. It is less about being wanted and more about being met. Less about validation and more about presence. This depth is not a diminishment. It is refinement. Desire becomes quieter, steadier, and more discerning. It values safety over novelty and truth over performance.

Desire without safety is anxiety.

Desire with safety is intimacy.

The work is not to resurrect desire through effort, but to create the conditions where it no longer needs to hide. These conditions are emotional honesty, bodily permission, and relational truth.

Intimacy in the second half of life is not about recreating the past. It is about telling the truth in the present. When women allow themselves this honesty, desire often returns as a quiet, steady form of aliveness. One that feels real, sustainable, and deeply connected to who they are now.

## Reflective Questions

1.  Where in your relationships do you feel most like you are performing rather than being?

2.  How have you learned to manage intimacy rather than experience it?

3.  What does safety feel like in your body, and where is it missing?

4.  How have cultural messages shaped what you believe about desire at this stage of life?

5.  Where might honesty deepen intimacy even if it initially creates discomfort?

6.  How does your body respond when your yes is fully chosen?

7.  What would it mean to allow desire to exist without apology or pressure?

# CHAPTER 11:
# MONEY AND POWER IN PARTNERSHIP

*"Power is not control over others;
it is the capacity to act with integrity."*

— Bell Hooks

She had not planned to bring up the question of whether she was still happy.

They were sitting at the kitchen table late in the evening, the house quiet in the way it only becomes after decades of shared life. The refrigerator hummed softly. A single overhead light cast long shadows across the wood grain.

Papers were spread between them: bank statements, a projected renovation cost, an upcoming investment decision. This was familiar territory. He leaned forward, calculator near his hand. She sat back slightly, pen resting idle against her notebook.

For years, this had been their choreography.

He managed the numbers.

She managed the atmosphere.

He projected.

She supported.

She had told herself it was efficient. He enjoyed financial strategy. She did not. It seemed practical to let him lead here.

But tonight, something felt different.

"Do we have enough?" she asked.

He looked up. "Of course we do," he replied quickly. "We're fine."

"That's not exactly what I meant."

He paused.

She studied the spreadsheets in front of them: columns of growth, percentages, security. On paper, their life was solid. Retirement funded. Investments diversified. No visible risk.

"I mean," she said carefully, "do we have enough for what I want next?"

Silence.

The question shifted the ground.

He blinked. "What do you want next?"

There it was, the real conversation.

For years, she had organized her desires around the perimeter of his financial decisions. Trips were framed as budgets. Projects were evaluated as returns. Even philanthropy had been structured strategically.

She had participated.

But she had not directed.

"I want to fund the mentorship program I've been thinking about," she said slowly, "without asking whether it's optimal. I want to feel like I can choose something because it matters to me, not because it performs well."

He leaned back now.

"I thought we were aligned," he said, not defensively, just surprised.

"We are," she replied. "But I'm not sure I've ever actually stepped into the power of deciding."

The air between them changed.

Money is rarely about money.

It is about voice.

About who sets direction.

About whose risk tolerance defines the horizon.

About whether partnership means shared authority or delegated control.

For decades, she had equated harmony with deference. He had equated leadership with protection. Neither had questioned the arrangement because it worked.

Until it didn't.

"Why didn't you say something before?" he asked.

She considered that.

"Because I didn't know I was allowed to."

That sentence landed heavier than any financial figure on the table.

In many long partnerships, especially in earlier generations, financial stewardship became synonymous with power. The one who controlled investments controlled pace. The one who analyzed risk defined possibility.

But mature partnership asks a different question:

Is power centralized or shared?

In the weeks that followed, they began revisiting more than spreadsheets. They revisited assumptions. He showed her the full architecture of their investments, not as a courtesy, but as transparency. She voiced desires without pre-editing them for feasibility.

There were awkward moments.

He had to release unilateral control.

She had to tolerate the discomfort of speaking into territory she had long ceded.

But something steadier emerged.

Not competition.

Alignment.

Power in partnership was no longer about who held the calculator.

It became about acting with integrity – together.

Money had always been his domain.

Not because he insisted, but because she had learned – slowly, subtly – that stepping back preserved harmony. He earned more. He tracked the accounts. He spoke with confidence. Over time, she stopped voicing her opinions unless asked. She told herself it didn't matter. That harmony mattered more.

But something in her body had changed over the past year. She had begun to notice when she went quiet. When her shoulders tightened. When she swallowed thoughts before they reached her mouth.

That night, as he began outlining what he thought they should do, she felt the familiar contraction – then something else.

A steadiness.

She interrupted him gently.

"I want to say something," she said. Her voice didn't shake, but it surprised them both.

Later that night, intimacy didn't arrive as obligation or routine. It emerged as connection. Eye contact lingered. Touch felt mutual rather than expected. Desire was not something she produced. It arose because she had not given herself away earlier in the evening.

Power had reorganized.

And desire followed.

She would later realize this was not about money alone.

It was about voice.

When financial power is unspoken, intimacy often compensates. One partner accommodates. The other remains unaware. Desire, in this landscape, becomes complicated, entangled with dependence, indebtedness, or quiet resentment.

But when money becomes a shared conversation rather than a silent hierarchy, something else becomes possible.

Equality does not guarantee desire.

But agency makes room for it.

Desire often returns not when finances are balanced, but when power is named and presence is restored.

Not all financial power imbalances follow traditional

lines. In some partnerships, the dynamic reverses – the woman becomes the primary earner, the financial engine, the visible driver of growth. On the surface, this appears progressive, even liberating. Yet when income shifts, identity often shifts with it. Provision carries psychological weight. Earning can quietly become authority. And even the most modern marriages are not immune to the subtle recalibrations that occur when money reorders influence. The question is not who earns more. The question is how power is interpreted when it does.

A couple of friends of mine, Lorrin and Joseph, navigated money from the opposite direction.

In this marriage, she earned more. Substantially more.

She had built a thriving consultancy. Her income fluctuated but consistently exceeded his steady salary. Early in their marriage, they had celebrated that fluidity: modern, equal, unthreatened.

But over time, subtle imbalances surfaced.

She felt pressure to sustain their lifestyle.

He felt diminished by comparison.

When large decisions arose – a new home, an investment, a philanthropic commitment – she often carried the final say, not because she insisted, but because her income anchored the choice.

"I don't want to feel like I'm asking permission for money I earned," she confessed one evening.

"And I don't want to feel like a junior partner in my life," he replied.

Different dynamic. Same issue.

Money had quietly become the measure of influence.

In their case, power did not reside in tradition. It resided in earnings.

They had to ask equally uncomfortable questions:

Is contribution only financial?

Does income define authority?

Can leadership rotate without destabilizing respect?

Their work required recalibration of ego, hers and his.

She had to disentangle competence from dominance.

He had to disentangle pride from provision.

They began defining "joint decisions" more explicitly. Thresholds for unilateral spending. Shared review of major investments. Transparent conversations about long-term security.

It was not romantic. It was adult.

Money in partnership reveals what we believe about worth.

About gender.

About contribution.

About entitlement.

In the second half of life, especially, these conversations become developmental milestones.

Because accumulated wealth magnifies imbalance if imbalance exists.

And security does not eliminate power dynamics. It clarifies them.

Both couples discovered something essential:

Financial harmony is not about equal earnings.

It is about equal agency.

It is about ensuring that neither silence nor dominance masquerades as peace.

In long marriages, money can calcify into structure, unquestioned, efficient, and unexamined.

But partnership matures when structure is revisited consciously.

Power, as bell hooks reminds us, is not control over others. It is the capacity to act with integrity.

In the second half of life, integrity requires visibility, even in the uncomfortable spaces of spreadsheets and silence.

Because when money and voice align, partnership deepens.

And when they do not, resentment quietly accrues interest.

When intimacy becomes performative, desire

withdraws.

Performance in intimacy is subtle. It does not usually look like deception. More often, it looks like accommodation. Anticipation. Emotional management. A woman learns to read her partner, sense expectations, and adjust herself accordingly. She becomes skilled at maintaining harmony, minimizing disruption, and preserving connection. Over time, intimacy becomes something she provides rather than something she inhabits.

Desire does not disappear in this process. It goes underground.

Many women interpret fading desire as a personal failure. They assume something is wrong with their bodies or their capacity for intimacy. They try to correct it through effort – reading, learning, pushing past reluctance, and overriding discomfort. These attempts rarely restore desire. They often deepen the disconnection.

Desire is not sustained by effort. It is sustained by safety.

Safety in intimacy is not predictability or routine. It is emotional truth. A woman feels safe when she does not have to manage her partner's reactions, protect the relationship from honesty, or suppress parts of herself to maintain closeness. When she can say no without consequence, express need without apology, and change without fear of abandonment, her body softens. Desire begins to stir.

Without safety, the body contracts. Desire retreats.

One woman described how her loss of desire unfolded gradually, almost imperceptibly. There was no defining moment, just a slow narrowing. She became careful. She prioritized peace. She avoided difficult conversations. Over time, intimacy felt scripted. Desire didn't vanish; it dulled.

When she began speaking more honestly, nothing dramatic happened at first. There was no sudden surge of passion. Instead, there was discomfort. Awkwardness. Uncertainty. Desire did not return as urgency, but as presence. She noticed herself breathing more deeply during conversations. Laughing more easily. Feeling her body again, not as an object of evaluation, but as a source of sensation.

Desire returned slowly, unevenly, and without performance. It felt sustainable because it was real.

But this is not the only path. Another woman experienced desire returning outside of partnership altogether.

After years of caretaking and emotional labor, she found herself disconnected not only from intimacy, but from pleasure itself. Her days were full, productive, and responsible. Her body felt efficient rather than alive. She assumed desire would return later, after rest, after resolution, after permission.

Instead, desire returned sideways. She began with small acts of attention. Walking without an agenda. Letting music fill her body rather than sit in the background. Choosing textures, flavors, movement for how they felt rather than how they appeared. There was no audience. No outcome. No one to manage.

At first, it felt unfamiliar, almost indulgent. Then it felt grounding.

Pleasure reintroduced her to herself.

Only later did she notice something else: her body felt more available. Not eager or urgent, but responsive. Desire was no longer something she owed or offered. It was something that arose when she felt present and unguarded.

Desire did not return because intimacy improved. Intimacy improved because desire reawakened within her. This distinction matters.

Desire does not always begin in relationship. Often, it begins with self-trust. In allowing the body to register sensation without evaluation. In reclaiming pleasure without justification. In lingering in warmth, sunlight, or stillness without needing to earn it.

Many women have learned that desire is disruptive,

indulgent, or inappropriate, especially in the second half of life. Cultural narratives often render women less visible, less expressive, less alive with age. These messages do not extinguish desire. They teach women to suppress it.

Over time, suppression becomes habit. Desire becomes dormant. Dormancy is not loss.

Reclaiming desire does not begin with action. It begins with honesty. What feels constraining? Where am I performing? What parts of myself have I muted to preserve harmony? These questions are not accusations. They are invitations.

Intimacy without authenticity is exhausting. Intimacy with authenticity is enlivening.

The difference is not technique. It is truth. When a woman allows herself to be seen as she is, by herself first, and then by others, desire becomes possible again. Not as pressure or performance, but as warmth. Curiosity. Presence.

Desire is not urgency. It is aliveness.

It does not demand constant expression. It asks for permission to exist. When a woman no longer apologizes for her wants or suppresses her no, desire feels less dangerous. It becomes integrated rather than explosive. It no longer needs to hide or rush.

This chapter is not an argument for constant intimacy or heightened sexuality. It is an argument for alignment. Desire reflects the state of connection – the connection a woman has with herself, and the connection she shares with another. When connection is honest, desire responds naturally. When it is managed, desire retreats.

In the second half of life, desire often becomes more discerning. Less about being wanted. More about being met. Less about validation. More about truth. This is not diminishment. It is refinement.

Desire without safety is anxiety. Desire with safety is intimacy.

The work is not to resurrect desire through effort, but

to create the conditions where it no longer needs to hide. These conditions are emotional honesty, bodily permission, and relational truth.

Intimacy in this season is not about recreating the past. It is about telling the truth in the present.

When women allow themselves this honesty, desire often returns, not loudly, but steadily, as a form of aliveness that feels real, sustainable, and deeply their own.

## Reflective Questions

1. Where in your relationships do you feel most like you are performing rather than being?

2. How have you learned to manage intimacy instead of experiencing it?

3. What does safety feel like in your body – and where is it missing?

4. How have cultural messages shaped what you believe about desire at this stage of life?

5. Where might honesty deepen intimacy, even if it initially creates discomfort?

6. How does your body respond when your yes is fully chosen?

7. What would it mean to allow desire to exist without apology or pressure?

# CHAPTER 12:
# WHEN CHOOSING YOURSELF DISRUPTS THE ROOM

*"You are the average of the five people
you spend the most time with."*

— Jim Rohn

I remember the first time I noticed the difference clearly.

It was a Thursday afternoon, and four of us had gathered at a small café with tall windows and uneven wooden floors in midtown Manhattan. Sunlight moved slowly across the table as we spoke. There were no phones face-up. No performative urgency. Just conversation.

"What are you building this year?" one woman asked, leaning forward with genuine interest.

Not *what are you managing* or *what are you surviving*, but building.

I shared an idea I had been shaping quietly, a Girls for STEM mentorship initiative, something that felt both purposeful and personal.

Instead of skepticism, I received curiosity.

"What would it look like if you didn't minimize it?" another asked.

"Who would it serve most powerfully?" a third added.

There was no competition in the room. No subtle recalibration of status. We spoke about health protocols we were experimenting with. Books that were stretching us. The tension between legacy and reinvention. One woman admitted she was rethinking a long-standing role she had held because it no longer felt aligned.

No one laughed at that.

We held it.

When I left, I felt energized, not stimulated, not flattered, but clearer. My spine felt straighter. My thinking more precise. I did not feel pressure to perform. I felt invited to expand.

Later that week, I met with another group of friends I had known for years.

We gathered in a familiar living room, comfortable, warm, layered with history. These were women who had walked with me through decades of life.

The conversation began predictably.

"Have you seen what they're doing now?" one woman said, shaking her head. "The world is just ridiculous."

Another chimed in. "And don't get me started on these younger women who think everything should be easy."

Laughter followed, not joyful, but bonding through dismissal.

I tried to introduce something that mattered to me.

"I've been thinking about stepping back from a few commitments," I offered. "I want to make room for something that feels more intentional."

There was a pause.

"Why?" one asked. "You've always thrived on being busy."

"I don't know," I said carefully. "It just doesn't feel aligned anymore."

"Aligned," someone repeated lightly, as if tasting the word. "You've been reading too many self-help books."

More laughter. It wasn't cruel. But it was constricting.

The conversation circled back, complaints about adult children not calling enough, irritation about aging bodies, resentment toward shifting cultural norms. The same grievances resurfaced with minor variations. Each attempt at reframing was gently neutralized.

"Well, that's just how it is."

"At our age, what do you expect?"

"Be careful. You don't want to isolate yourself chasing growth."

There it was.

Growth reframed as threat.

As naïveté.

As disloyalty to shared narrative.

When I left that evening, I felt heavy.

Not because they were unkind.

Because I had edited myself.

I had softened language. Minimized desire. Avoided mentioning what truly energized me. I had matched tone rather than holding truth.

Belonging had required compression.

The specific complaint that kept circling that night was about relevance.

"No one listens to women our age anymore," one said. "We've done our part," another added. "Now it's just maintenance."

Maintenance.

The word lingered.

In the first gathering, we spoke about becoming.

In the second, we spoke about enduring.

The contrast was not about intelligence or loyalty.

It was about orientation.

One group asked, *What are you still capable of?*

The other implied, *This is as far as it goes.*

And here is the difficult truth:

When you begin choosing yourself, choosing alignment, growth, vitality, it disrupts rooms organized around resignation. Your expansion highlights their contraction. Your hope challenges their cynicism. Your refusal to shrink can feel, to others, like quiet betrayal. The discomfort is not because you are wrong. It is because systems of belonging are delicate.

If a group bonds around shared frustration, introducing possibility alters the chemistry. The question this chapter explores is not whether you abandon long-standing friendships. It is whether you continue contorting yourself to preserve them.

Because eventually, you must decide: Is belonging worth self-reduction? Or can you withstand the discomfort of being the woman in the room who is still becoming?

That contrast was clarifying.

Choosing myself did not mean judging anyone or announcing distance. It meant becoming more honest about where my energy went, and why. It meant recognizing that not every longstanding relationship is meant to accompany every season of life.

This is often where choosing yourself becomes relationally complicated.

The book explores autonomy, boundaries, rest, truth, and self-trust. Yet for many women, the real friction does not arise in private decisions. It arises in relationships. Growth does not happen in isolation. It happens inside families, partnerships, friendships, and communities that were shaped around who you used to be.

When a woman becomes more selective with her time and energy, others notice. Friends may interpret this as withdrawal or judgment. They may say, "You've changed," with uncertainty or disappointment. What they are often responding to is not rejection, but recalibration.

What I began to understand is that energy is information.

As women age, tolerance for emotional depletion decreases. This is not selfishness. It is discernment. The nervous system becomes less willing to sustain relationships that require constant management, chronic criticism, or self-betrayal. Time feels more precious. Presence feels more valuable. Choosing relationships that uplift, challenge, and support growth becomes a form of self-respect rather than preference.

This selectivity can be misread.

Friends accustomed to unlimited access may feel excluded. Those who relied on you for emotional labor may feel unsettled. The absence of your previous availability can be experienced as loss, even if nothing explicit has been taken away.

This same dynamic appears in families and partnerships.

When a partner interprets your need for space as rejection, it can trigger fear. When adult children experience new boundaries as abandonment, it can provoke guilt. When loved ones are accustomed to your responsiveness, your steadiness may feel unfamiliar or even threatening.

Discomfort does not mean harm. It means the nervous system registers the strain long before the mind admits it.

Many relationships are built on unspoken agreements. Who listens. Who absorbs tension. Who makes things easier. When a woman steps out of a role she has long inhabited, the structure shifts. What once felt stable becomes uncertain, not because it was healthy, but because it was predictable.

This is where many women hesitate. They wonder if they are being selfish. If they are withdrawing rather than evolving. If choosing themselves means choosing against others.

It does not.

Choosing yourself means choosing from a place that is no longer internally divided. It means allowing your relationships to reorganize around who you are now, rather than who you needed to be before.

Compassion does not require self-abandonment.

You can acknowledge that change is difficult without undoing the change. You can hold space for someone's disappointment without rushing to repair it. You can remain kind without returning to patterns that depleted you.

Over time, some relationships deepen.

Friends who are aligned with your values often rise into clearer focus. Conversations become more meaningful. Mutual support replaces obligation. You no longer need to explain why growth matters to you. It is understood.

Other relationships loosen or complete. This is not failure. It is sorting.

Not every connection is meant to travel the full distance of your life. Releasing a relationship does not negate what it once offered. It honors the truth that change reshapes us in ways not every connection can accommodate.

Choosing yourself does not harden the heart. It clarifies it.

When you remain grounded, consistent, and present, many people eventually adjust. They come to trust that your boundaries are not punishment, but orientation. And when they do not, your steadiness still matters. It protects your energy. It preserves your integrity. It allows you to live truthfully without needing consensus.

This chapter is not an invitation to cut people off or withdraw from love. It is an invitation to choose relationships that sustain rather than drain, that invite expansion rather than contraction, that support the life you are building now.

When you choose yourself, the room will feel different. Some will lean in. Some will step back. Some will need time.

None of this means you are doing it wrong.

It means you are listening.

## Reflective Questions

1. Where in your life do you notice a clear difference between relationships that energize

2. What beliefs make it difficult for you to be selective about where you spend your time and emotional energy?

3. How do you typically respond when others interpret your boundaries as rejection or withdrawal?

4. Which roles have you played in friendships or family relationships that no longer feel aligned?

5. Where are you tempted to over-explain or justify your choices rather than remain steady?

6. What qualities do the relationships that support your growth share in common?

7. How might your life feel if you trusted discernment rather than guilt when choosing where to invest your energy?

# CHAPTER 13:
# WHY MEN THRIVE BESIDE A SEASONED WOMAN

*"The greatest gift one partner can offer
another is not perfection, but presence."*

— David Whyte

My friend Ruben described how his partner's clarity initially unsettled him. For years, Gloria had been the emotional interpreter in their relationship. If tension arose at work, she softened it. If conflict surfaced between them, she translated his frustration into language he could tolerate. If he withdrew, she reached. If he reacted, she absorbed.

He had not thought of it as imbalance. He thought of it as harmony.

Then something changed.

Gloria became less available to absorb stress that was not hers. When he came home agitated, she listened, but she did not immediately soothe. When he spoke sharply, she did not rush to reframe it for him. When decisions arose that were his to make, she declined to step in and organize them.

"She used to buffer everything," he said. "And suddenly... she didn't."

At first, Ruben felt exposed.

Conversations that once ended quickly now lingered. Discomfort remained in the room instead of dissolving. There was no emotional cushioning, no gentle translation of his mood into something more digestible.

"It felt like she'd pulled the padding off the walls," he admitted. "I didn't realize how much I leaned on her to manage the atmosphere."

Without her reflexive smoothing, he had to sit with his irritation. Name his fears. Clarify his requests.

Ruben interpreted the shift as withdrawal.

"Are you okay?" he asked her one evening. "You seem... distant."

"I'm not distant," Gloria replied calmly. "I'm just not carrying what isn't mine anymore."

The sentence unsettled him.

Not because it was harsh.

Because it was accurate.

For a time, he felt slightly destabilized. The ease he had grown accustomed to required more effort from him now. He had to regulate himself. He had to articulate rather than assume she would infer. He had to own decisions rather than defer subtly.

Growth rarely feels comfortable at first.

But over time, something unexpected happened.

Ruben began to feel respected.

Not managed.

Not corrected.

Not parented.

Respected.

Gloria's clarity communicated something powerful: *I believe you can carry your interior life.*

Without her emotional over-functioning, he stepped more fully into his steadiness. He learned to pause before reacting. To express frustration without outsourcing its management. To tolerate silence without interpreting it as abandonment.

"The relationship became more direct," he said. "Less

padded. But more honest."

There was less choreography. More truth.

He felt more fully himself – not because she demanded change, but because she no longer shielded him from it.

Goria's refusal to cushion was not punishment.

It was partnership.

And in that partnership, power recalibrated.

Not as control.

But as mutual responsibility.

When a woman enters the second half of life with greater self-trust, clarity, and boundaries, something subtle but unmistakable shifts in her relationships with men. This shift is often misunderstood by partners who sense it, and by women who are still adjusting to their authority.

It is not about dominance, emotional withdrawal, or independence for its own sake. It is about coherence. And coherence reshapes relational dynamics in ways that are both quiet and profound.

A seasoned woman is no longer organizing her life around approval. She is less inclined to manage emotions, anticipate needs before they are spoken, or perform steadiness in order to preserve harmony. She is not less caring or less engaged. She is more honest. This honesty alters the relational field. Men often respond not because they are being corrected or challenged, but because the dynamic has shifted. She is no longer preemptively managing emotion or preserving harmony at her expense.

Many men thrive beside seasoned women because pressure is reduced. When a woman stops unconsciously performing emotional labor, men are invited into greater responsibility without being shamed into it. When she no longer over-functions, men are not diminished. They are called into fuller responsibility.

This chapter is not an argument about gender superiority. It is about relational maturity.

In many partnerships, imbalance arises not from malice or neglect, but from accommodation. Women learn early to smooth, manage, translate, and adapt. Men learn to rely on this without necessarily choosing it consciously. Over time, both partners become constrained by these patterns. The woman may feel depleted or unseen. The man may feel subtly disconnected from his emotional authority. When a woman steps out of these roles, the system must reorganize.

Seasoned women do not rescue men from discomfort. They trust men's capacity to grow through it. This trust is often deeply attractive. It communicates respect rather than control. It allows men to step forward without defensiveness or shame.

Men also thrive because seasoned women bring less urgency into relationship. Having confronted time, loss, and identity, they are less driven by anxiety around outcomes. They are less likely to rush intimacy or avoid difficult conversations. They can tolerate pauses. They can remain present during conflict without escalating or collapsing. This steadiness creates safety that does not depend on constant reassurance.

This does not mean seasoned women are passive or endlessly patient. In fact, they are often more direct than they have ever been. What has softened is the need to persuade, justify, or convince. Boundaries are clearer. Expectations are spoken rather than implied. Men often respond well to this clarity. It removes ambiguity. It replaces emotional guesswork with truth.

Another man described how his partner's refusal to over explain changed everything. Instead of debating feelings or defending her needs, she stated them calmly. He found himself listening more closely. The relationship became less performative and more grounded. He was no longer responding to urgency or reactivity. He was responding to presence.

Seasoned women also change how power operates in partnership. Because they no longer equate love with self sacrifice, power becomes shared rather than negotiated through guilt, obligation, or silent resentment. Men are no longer positioned as providers or protectors by default. They are partners. Responsibility becomes mutual rather than assumed.

This shift relieves men of narrow roles. It allows them to be vulnerable without losing dignity. To contribute without carrying everything. To be met rather than managed. When women stop managing outcomes, men are free to show up more fully.

Importantly, men do not thrive beside seasoned women because women become easier. They thrive because women become truer. Truth creates resonance. Resonance invites reciprocity. There is less performance on both sides and more authenticity in the space between.

This chapter is not a prescription for how women should behave in order to support men. It is an observation of what often happens when women stop contorting themselves to preserve relationship. Men who are willing to grow frequently respond with greater presence, engagement, and respect.

Not all relationships survive this shift. Some are built on imbalance that cannot withstand mutuality. This is not a failure. It is information. Where growth is reciprocal, connection deepens. Where it is not, clarity emerges.

Seasoned women no longer ask whether they are too much or not enough. They ask whether the relationship can meet them where they are. Men who can answer yes often discover that partnership feels less burdensome and more alive.

Ultimately, men flourish beside women who are not performing, rescuing, or shrinking. They flourish beside women who know themselves, trust themselves, and allow partnership to be a place of mutual evolution rather than emotional labor.

When one person grows, the relationship must respond. Men who rise to that moment often discover that intimacy feels steadier, lighter, and more real.

## Reflective Questions

1. How have your relationships with men shifted as you have become clearer about your needs, boundaries, and truth?

2. In what ways have you historically over functioned in relationships to preserve harmony or avoid conflict?

3. How do men in your life respond when you stop managing emotional outcomes or smoothing discomfort?

4. Where do you notice relief when you allow others to carry responsibility?

5. What does mutual responsibility look like in your current partnerships, emotionally, practically, and relationally?

6. Where does clarity feel more respectful and stabilizing than accommodation or self sacrifice?

7. Which relationships feel strengthened by your growth, and which feel strained by it?

8. What beliefs about love or partnership make it difficult to trust that truth invites reciprocity?

9. How might your relationships change if you trusted that being fully yourself is not a threat to connection?

What would it mean to let partnership be a space of shared evolution rather than emotional labor?

# INTERLUDE:
# A LETTER TO THE WOMAN I USED TO BE

Some words are written forward. Others are written backward, across time. This letter belongs to both directions.

I did not sit down one day and decide to write to you. These words accumulated quietly, through years of living, choosing, losing, and arriving. They gathered in moments I did not mark as significant at the time, in decisions made without certainty, in strength borrowed from women who came before me, before it was fully earned, in endurance mistaken for purpose. Nothing about this letter is strategic. It is the residue of experience, what remained after urgency softened and effort loosened its grip.

I see you now more clearly than I could then. I see how much you carried without naming the weight. How often you translated yourself to be understood, adjusted yourself to be accepted, and moved quickly because slowing felt dangerous. You believed responsibility was proof of worth. You believed resilience required silence. You believed arrival would feel obvious when it happened. None of this was wrong. It was how you survived, how you built, how you loved.

This letter is not an apology, and it is not a correction.

It is a recognition. You did what you knew how to do with the information you had.

You were not failing. You were becoming. You were learning through motion what could not yet be learned through reflection. The clarity I carry now was shaped by the choices you made then, even the ones that cost you something.

I am not here despite you. I am here because of you.

So, this letter ends not with instruction or regret, but with gratitude. You carried what I no longer need to hold. You walked so I could arrive. And I honor you, not by rewriting your path, but by living what you made possible.

## Letter to the Woman I'm Becoming

I see you ahead of me.

Not as someone perfected, but as someone more at ease in her skin. More deliberate. Less hurried by expectation. I feel you in the quiet choices I am beginning to make – the pauses I take, the boundaries I honor, the honesty I no longer postpone.

You are not built on urgency.

For years, strength meant holding things together. Anticipating what might go wrong. Reading the room before entering it. Carrying more than was assigned so that others could feel steady. That strength shaped me. It taught me competence, resilience, discernment.

But you are not defined by how much you can carry.

You are defined by how honestly you live.

There was a time when effort felt like safety. When proving felt like progress. When exhaustion was misnamed devotion. I understand why that season existed. It formed muscle and endurance. It sharpened awareness. It built a life.

But you are not meant to live in constant reinforcement.

As I move toward you, I am learning to loosen my grip. To speak needs without over-explaining. To say no without rehearsing guilt. To allow silence without rushing to fill it.

You do not harden to remain strong.

You soften to remain whole.

When I feel the old reflex to manage emotion or smooth discomfort, I pause. When I sense myself performing steadiness rather than inhabiting it, I breathe. Each time I choose alignment over approval, I feel closer to you.

You are a woman who no longer organizes her life around being needed. You are steady without overextending. Present without performing. Honest without aggression. You allow relationships to adjust rather than contort yourself to preserve them.

Desire, in you, is not urgency. It is warmth. Curiosity. Aliveness that does not need to justify its existence.

You trust yourself.

You do not chase relevance; you embody it. You do not argue for space; you inhabit it. You do not over-function to prove love; you offer presence and allow others to meet you there.

I am not striving to become you.

I am shedding what prevents me from arriving.

The years behind me were not wasted. They were formative. They taught me what endurance cannot teach forever – that strength without softness becomes strain, and responsibility without alignment becomes erosion.

As I move forward, I choose coherence. I choose steadiness that does not exhaust me. I choose truth over harmony when harmony costs integrity.

I am becoming you – not by adding more, but by releasing what no longer aligns.

And I welcome the woman who walks beside me now: steady, present, and fully herself.

# CHAPTER 14:
# REST AS INTELLIGENCE

*"Your body is not an obstacle to your purpose;
it is the place where wisdom arrives."*

— Richard Rohr

For many women who have lived lives of responsibility and achievement, rest has been misunderstood. It has been framed as recovery after depletion, a concession to limitation, or a pause earned only after usefulness has been exhausted. Rest has often been treated as optional, something to fit in once everything else has been handled.

For many women, rest has been treated as reward. Something granted after enough effort, after enough usefulness, after enough visible contribution. It has been framed as recovery – a pause to repair what life has depleted.

But that framing is incomplete.

What is rarely recognized is this:

Rest is not recovery from life.

It is intelligence within it.

Rest is not withdrawal from responsibility. It is the recalibration that allows responsibility to remain humane. It is how the nervous system integrates experience. How clarity returns. How desire resurfaces without force.

In my writing and research on longevity, particularly in

my books, *Longevity: Reinvent Yourself at Any Age* and *Designing Your Longevity*, I emphasize that the body is not separate from purpose or productivity. It is the medium through which clarity, vitality, and meaning are sustained. The body is always communicating. The question is not whether it speaks, but whether we listen.

For a long time, I didn't.

## When the Body Is Finally Forced to Speak

There were signs before the

crisis: a persistent tightness beneath my right ribcage that I dismissed as indigestion; a heaviness after meals that I attributed to stress; fatigue that lingered longer than it should have. I adjusted my diet slightly, drank more water, took antacids, shifted appointments. I told myself I was managing it.

I had always managed things.

That morning began like many others.

I woke early, already mentally outlining the day: emails to return, a call scheduled mid-morning, notes I wanted to revise. I remember standing in the kitchen with a cup of coffee, feeling a dull ache just below my ribs.

"Probably something I ate," I muttered.

I ate lightly, moved through the morning, took a call while standing at my desk, pacing slightly as I spoke. The discomfort intensified – not sharp, but insistent.

By early afternoon, it had sharpened.

A wave of nausea followed. I sat down, then stood up again, unable to find a position that eased it. I told myself it would pass.

It did not.

The pain spread across my abdomen and into my back, tightening like a band being drawn inward. I leaned against the kitchen counter and closed my eyes.

This is when denial begins to crack.

I called my husband.

"I think something's wrong," I said quietly, trying to

sound composed.

He heard it immediately.

"I'm coming home."

By the time he arrived, I was bent slightly forward, breathing shallowly, sweat gathering along my hairline. The drive to the hospital is blurred in my memory, but I remember gripping the door handle, trying to remain upright as each bump in the road sent a surge through my body.

There is a particular vulnerability in needing to be driven.

For decades, I had been the one who drove others, organized care, managed emergencies, held steadiness.

Now I was the one in pain.

At the emergency room, the fluorescent lights felt harsh. Questions were asked quickly, pain levels assessed, blood drawn, an ultrasound ordered.

I lay on a narrow bed, staring at ceiling tiles while machines hummed around me.

The diagnosis came without

drama: gallstones, inflammation. Surgery recommended immediately.

Within hours, I was being wheeled into an operating room.

There is a moment before anesthesia when the body understands what the mind is still catching up to.

This is not inconvenience.

This is intervention.

When I woke in recovery, groggy and hollowed out, the clarity was stark.

This was not bad luck.

It was cumulative.

Years of pushing through discomfort. Years of overriding subtle signals. Years of translating bodily whispers into productivity strategies.

The body had been speaking.

I had been fluent in everything except its language.

Lying in that hospital bed, I felt something deeper than pain.

I felt consequence.

Not punishment.

Consequence.

The gallbladder does not inflame overnight. It responds to long patterns – stress chemistry, suppressed tension, metabolic overload.

The crisis was dramatic.

The pattern had been quiet.

And that is when rest reframed itself for me.

Rest is not collapse.

It is intelligence.

Rest is not earned after exhaustion.

It is responsiveness before rupture.

Longevity is not endurance.

It is attunement.

In the days following surgery, moving slowly through my home, I began to understand something foundational:

The body will negotiate.

Until it won't.

And when it stops negotiating, it speaks volumes.

That hospital bed became the origin point for how I now understand the five types of rest: physical, emotional, cognitive, relational, and spiritual. Each one is a form of early listening. Each one interrupts accumulation before it becomes crisis.

If I had honored physical rest earlier, perhaps inflammation would not have escalated.

If I had honored emotional rest, not absorbing what was not mine, perhaps my nervous system would not have remained in chronic vigilance.

If I had honored cognitive rest, less constant processing, less mental rehearsal, perhaps my body chemistry would have softened.

The surgery removed an organ.

But it also removed denial.

And from that moment forward, rest stopped being optional.

It became strategy.

That experience changed how I understand rest, not as indulgence or recovery, but as early intervention. My body had been asking for attention long before it demanded it. I had simply been too skilled at overriding the signals.

Longevity is not about endurance. It is about responsiveness.

Rest as Intelligence, Not Collapse

The body does not wait for burnout or illness to communicate. Long before crisis arrives, it signals through irritability that cannot be explained, through shallow sleep, chronic tension, diminished pleasure, and a loss of ease. These signals are not failures of discipline or strength. They are information.

The body does not speak in arguments or logic. It speaks in sensation.

Many women – especially those who have succeeded through responsibility, caregiving, and resilience – are exceptionally good at ignoring these signals. This capacity has enabled extraordinary lives. It has also required disconnection. Over time, the body becomes something to manage rather than something to consult.

The cost of this disconnection is subtle at first. Clarity narrows. Desire dulls. Decision-making becomes reactive rather than discerning. Life begins to feel heavier – not because it is harder, but because it is being carried without adequate support.

When we begin to see rest as intelligence, fatigue no longer signals weakness. It signals guidance. It asks a different question:

*Not how do I recover so I can continue as before, but what is my body telling me about how I am living now?*

This question invites a new relationship with the body, one based not on dominance or discipline, but on collaboration.

## The Five Types of Rest: A Practical Framework for Listening Sooner

Rest is not singular. Different forms of depletion require different forms of restoration. Many women attempt to resolve all exhaustion with sleep alone. While physical rest is essential, it is often insufficient.

Understanding which type of rest is needed allows women to respond precisely rather than reactively.

### 1. Physical Rest

Physical rest addresses the body's need for sleep, nourishment, recovery, and reduced exertion. Without it, the nervous system remains taxed. Yet many women discover that even with more sleep, fatigue persists – signaling other forms of depletion.

### 2. Mental Rest

Mental rest is needed when the mind is in constant motion – planning, anticipating, deciding, evaluating, managing outcomes. Mental rest occurs when thought is released from productivity. Silence, repetition, time in nature, or creative immersion allow the mind to settle.

### 3. Emotional Rest

Emotional rest becomes necessary when a woman carries more emotional responsibility than she receives – when she is consistently the listener, the stabilizer, the one who absorbs tension. Emotional rest happens when she is not required to explain herself, manage reactions, or remain composed for others' comfort.

### 4. Sensory Rest

Sensory rest is essential in environments saturated with noise, screens, stimulation, and urgency. The nervous system cannot recalibrate without quiet. Sensory rest allows the body to return to baseline. Without it, the body remains on alert even during stillness.

### *5. Spiritual Rest*

Spiritual rest addresses the deeper need for meaning, coherence, and truth beyond obligation. Without it, life can feel full but uninhabited – busy, productive, and strangely empty. Spiritual rest is restored in moments that reconnect a woman to what feels essential: in solitude without agenda; in prayer or meditation that is not performance; in time spent in nature where nothing is required of her; in conversations that allow depth rather than efficiency; in rituals that mark transition and return her to herself.

It is not about productivity. It is about remembering.

When these forms of rest are understood, fatigue becomes informative rather than discouraging. Instead of pushing harder or collapsing indiscriminately, women can listen and adjust.

In longevity work, this distinction matters deeply. Extending life without restoring coherence simply prolongs depletion. True longevity requires alignment – between body, values, energy, and purpose.

## Authority Through Listening

Rest restores clarity because it reopens access to internal signals. When a woman is chronically depleted, everything feels urgent. Boundaries blur. Choices feel heavy. When rest is integrated intentionally, discernment returns. What once felt confusing becomes obvious.

Rest is also a form of authority.

In a culture that rewards endurance and constant output, choosing rest requires self-trust. It means valuing internal wisdom over external metrics. It means rejecting the belief that worth is proven through exhaustion.

After success, this shift becomes unavoidable. The strategies that once fueled achievement no longer sustain well-being. The body demands a different rhythm. Ignoring this demand leads to illness, resentment, or collapse. Responding to it leads to coherence.

Rest does not make women less capable.

It makes them more precise.

Many women find they do less, but with greater impact. Life becomes intentional rather than reactive. Longevity becomes not just about years lived, but about years inhabited.

The body is not something to overcome.

It is something to consult.

I learned that lesson in a hospital room I never expected to be in. I now teach it so others might listen sooner than I did.

When women enter partnership with their bodies, vitality stabilizes, clarity deepens, and life becomes sustainable again, not through endurance, but through intelligence.

## Reflective Questions

1. How were you taught to think about rest earlier in your life – reward, weakness, or necessity?

2. What signals has your body been giving you that you may have minimized or ignored?

3. Which forms of rest do you most often neglect: physical, mental, emotional, sensory, or spiritual?

4. How does your decision-making change when you are well-rested versus depleted?

5. Where might listening sooner prevent a larger interruption later?

6. What would a more collaborative relationship with your body look like now?

7. How might honoring rest reshape not only your health, but your approach to longevity and purpose?

# CHAPTER 15:
# ALIVENESS IN THE PRESENCE OF LOSS



*"The wound is the place where the Light enters you."*

— Rumi

This season of life includes loss. Not as an exception, but as part of the terrain. Bodies change. Capacities narrow. Illness enters uninvited. People we love decline, disappear, or die. Futures we assumed quietly dissolve. Any invitation to aliveness that does not make room for these realities risks feeling superficial.

To be alive in this season is not to be spared from loss. It is to learn how to hold it without disappearing yourself.

Many women reach this point carrying grief they have never fully named. Not only grief for loved ones lost, but grief for health that no longer feels reliable, for energy that must be rationed, for a body that no longer responds to willpower alone. There is grief in realizing that time is finite in a way that can no longer be intellectualized.

Loss arrives in different forms.

For some, it comes through illness. A diagnosis that changes the body's terms. A procedure that leaves behind a permanent adjustment. A condition that demands vigilance and humility rather than control. The body becomes less abstract and more authoritative. It demands to be listened to.

For others, loss comes through caregiving. Watching a parent, a partner, or a loved one fade in ways that cannot be fixed. Alzheimer's is particularly devastating in this regard. It does not only take memory. It takes recognition, reciprocity, and shared narrative. The person you love is still here, but no longer fully reachable in the ways that once anchored you.

While writing *Stolen Memories: A Journey Through Alzheimer's*, I came to understand something no theory had prepared me for.

Loss does not arrive all at once. It arrives in increments.

One afternoon, I sat beside Claire, as late sunlight filtered through half-drawn curtains. The room was quiet except for the TV.

I knelt slightly so she could see me clearly.

"Hi, Claire," I said gently. "It's Maria."

She turned toward me slowly. Her eyes rested on my face with effort, not blank, not cold, simply searching. I watched the recognition try to assemble itself behind her gaze.

It didn't.

Instead, she smiled politely.

"Are you visiting?" she asked.

There is a particular tenderness in that question.

I felt the familiar internal drop, the small grief that never fully dulls. Claire, my mother-in-law, who had once known me through holidays, conversations, shared history, now met me as a stranger.

"Yes," I replied. "I am."

I did not correct her. I did not insist on memory.

I sat beside her.

We spoke about the light coming through the window. About the way the trees were moving outside. For a moment, identity loosened. We were not bound by titles – mother-in-law, daughter-in-law – or by the architecture of shared history.

We were simply present.

Then, unexpectedly, she looked at me and said, "You have kind eyes."

The sentence pierced me.

She did not know my name.

But she recognized my presence.

Later, when Stephen entered and teased her about always being strong-willed, she surprised us both with a quick reply.

"Someone had to be," she said, her mouth lifting in that familiar flash of wit.

We laughed.

Not because the disease had retreated. But because something essential remained.

That afternoon reshaped my understanding of identity. Alzheimer's strips memory, language, narrative continuity, the very structures we use to define who we are. It reveals how much of our identity we attach to story, competence, relational roles.

And yet, beneath those layers, something persists. Tone. Warmth. Humor. A certain way of looking at the world. Presence.

Watching Claire lose cognitive scaffolding forced me to confront an uncomfortable question:

If memory dissolves, what remains of the self? The answer was not productivity.

Not achievement. Not titles. It was essence.

That experience altered how I understood my life. For years, I had measured vitality through accomplishment, through contribution, leadership, output. But sitting at that bedside, I saw that when everything performative falls away, what endures is not what you built.

It is how you are.

How you sit beside someone. How you listen. How

you carry calm into a room.

Alzheimer's taught me that identity is not secured by performance. It is revealed in presence.

And that realization informed everything that followed, my understanding of longevity, of rest, of the second half of life. Longevity is not simply the extension of years. It is the preservation of essence. Rest is not retreat from usefulness. It is protection of presence.

When I later found myself overriding my fatigue, ignoring subtle bodily signals, pushing past discomfort in the name of discipline, I remembered Claire. I remembered how fragile the scaffolding of function can be.

I remembered how little achievement matters when consciousness narrows to a single afternoon of sunlight and breath.

It changed my pace. It softened my urgency.

It made rest feel less like indulgence and more like reverence — reverence for the body, the nervous system, the limited and precious architecture that allows us to show up in the world at all.

Alzheimer's does not only teach us about loss. It teaches us about essence. And essence does not need to prove. It needs to be protected.

And yet, even here, aliveness remains possible.

Not as cheerfulness. Not as denial. But as presence.

Aliveness in the presence of loss looks different. It is quieter. More deliberate. It does not demand that grief resolve itself before life is allowed to continue. It lets sorrow and vitality coexist.

My friend Lorrin described sitting beside her husband as his illness progressed. Their conversations shortened. Plans disappeared. The future narrowed. At first, she felt herself shrinking along with it. Later, something shifted. She began noticing small moments with an intensity she had not known before: the warmth of his hand, the rhythm of shared silence, the way light moved across the room in the late afternoon. Her life became smaller in scope, but deeper in texture.

This was not resignation. It was attention.

My sister Zulema spoke of her health limitations after years of pushing through pain. She could no longer travel the way she once had. Her stamina was unpredictable. At first, she experienced this as loss of identity. Who was she without her former capacity? Over time, she began designing her days differently. In redesigning her days, she discovered that capacity had changed, but worth had not.

These insights echo themes I explored in my books, *Longevity: Reinvent Yourself at Any Age* and *Designing Your Longevity*, where the goal is not endless extension, but sustainable presence. Longevity, in its truest sense, is not about avoiding decline at all costs. It is about staying in relationship with life as it changes.

Loss also brings mortality closer.

Friends fall ill. Partners age. Death moves from abstraction to proximity. This awareness can be destabilizing, but it can also clarify. Many women report that after significant loss, trivial concerns lose their grip. The appetite for pretense diminishes. What matters sharpens.

Aliveness becomes less about accumulation and more about intimacy with the moment.

This does not mean grief is resolved or pain is redeemed. Loss is not made meaningful by endurance alone. What changes is orientation. Instead of waiting for life to return to what it was, a woman begins to meet life where it is.

Presence becomes an act of courage.

In *The Consciousness Blueprint*, I wrote about presence as the ground state that emerges when internal conflict quiets. Loss accelerates this process. It strips away illusion. It leaves less room for distraction. When a woman allows herself to be present even in pain, she often discovers that presence does not abandon her in return.

Aliveness here may look like choosing one nourishing conversation instead of many obligations. It may look like honoring the body's limits without resentment. It may look like grieving fully without rushing toward resolution. It may look like laughter that surprises you, not because loss has vanished, but because life insists on showing up anyway.

This chapter does not suggest that loss is a teacher to be grateful for. It suggests that loss is a reality to be met honestly. Aliveness is not diminished by acknowledging mortality. It is intensified.

To be alive in this season is to know that time matters and to live accordingly. It is to love without guarantees. To care without control. To remain awake even when the future feels uncertain.

This is not optimism. It is courage.

The invitation of this book has always been toward aliveness that is earned, not performed. Aliveness that includes rest, truth, boundaries, pleasure, discernment, and now, grief. When all of these are allowed to coexist, life becomes more real, not less.

Loss will come. In some form, it already has.

The question is not whether you will grieve. The question is whether you will allow yourself to live fully while you do.

## Reflective Questions

1. What forms of loss have shaped this season of your life, whether through health, caregiving, or the death of someone you love?

2. How have illness or physical limitations changed your relationship with your body and your expectations of yourself?

3. Where do you notice grief asking for space rather than resolution?

4. What helps you feel alive even in the presence of sorrow?

5. How has awareness of mortality clarified what matters most to you now?

6.  Where might you be postponing aliveness until loss feels "resolved?"

7.  What would it mean to let grief and vitality coexist without forcing either to disappear?

# CHAPTER 16:
# THE NERVOUS SYSTEM KNOWS

*"The body is our first language."*

— Stephen Porges

Before you read another sentence, pause. Let your eyes lift from the page.

Notice your jaw. Is it lightly resting, or is it subtly engaged? Let your tongue drop from the roof of your mouth. Allow your shoulders to descend, not dramatically, just enough to feel gravity.

Now lengthen your exhale.

Do not force the inhale. Simply let the exhale take a second longer than usual. As if you are fogging a mirror gently.

Notice what changes.

Perhaps your chest softens. Perhaps your stomach releases slightly. Perhaps nothing obvious happens at all.

But something has shifted.

Your nervous system just registered safety.

This is the body's first intelligence.

Long before thought, before language, before narrative, your nervous system is scanning the environment and asking a single, quiet question:

Am I safe enough to settle?

If the answer is uncertain, the body prepares.

The breath becomes shallow.

The jaw firms.

The shoulders brace.

The mind sharpens.

This is not dysfunction. It is design.

The nervous system has three broad responses available: mobilize, immobilize, or connect. Stephen Porges' polyvagal theory gives language to what we feel instinctively. When we sense safety, the social engagement system activates. We feel open, curious, relational. When we sense threat, even subtle threat, the body mobilizes into fight or flight. When overwhelm becomes too great, it can shut down entirely.

The body does not wait for your interpretation.

It moves first.

For years, I lived in a narrow band of chronic activation and called it competence.

I could read rooms quickly, anticipate tension, stay alert, and manage complexity without visible strain. I thought I was disciplined.

But discipline and vigilance are not the same.

My breath rarely dropped fully into my abdomen. My shoulders rested slightly elevated, as if prepared for impact. Even in calm settings, my nervous system remained poised.

I was not in crisis. I was in readiness.

The problem is not acute stress. It is sustained micro-activation, the kind that never escalates enough to alarm you, but never resolves enough to restore you.

The gallbladder surgery was dramatic. But the nervous system story began long before that day. The body had been whispering through tension, fatigue, and digestive disruption. I translated those whispers as inconvenience. They were intelligence.

Rest, then, is not collapse. It is a return to regulation.

Try this: Place one hand over your sternum and one over your lower ribs. Take a slow inhale through your nose. Let your lower hand move first, then your upper. On the exhale, let both hands fall naturally.

Do this three times.

Notice if your mind resists the simplicity of it.

Notice if you feel impatient.

That impatience is also information.

In the second half of life, we are invited into a more refined listening.

Not listening for catastrophe. Listening for subtlety.

Does this conversation tighten your chest?

Does this obligation shorten your breath?

Does this environment soften you or constrict you?

The nervous system knows before your calendar does.

Presence is not a mindset. It is a physiological state.

When your body feels safe, your thoughts become clearer, your voice steadier, your boundaries more precise. You are less reactive, more responsive.

Longevity is not about enduring more stress. It is about restoring more often. The difference between performance and presence is measurable in the body.

Performance requires activation. Presence requires regulation.

The work now is not to push harder. It is to notice sooner. Your body is not an obstacle to your purpose. It is the instrument through which purpose is lived. And it has been speaking to you all along.

By now, you may have noticed a pattern running quietly through this book: the movement from performance to presence, from compulsion to coherence.

Rest restores clarity. Boundaries bring relief. Desire responds to safety. Time feels scarce when life is rushed and spacious when it is settled. These shifts are not philosophical alone. They are physiological.

Long before conscious thought forms, the nervous system is already responding.

It is continuously evaluating safety, threat, connection, and capacity. It shapes how we breathe, how we listen, how we respond to conflict, and how we experience intimacy. It influences whether we feel open or guarded, present or rushed, alive or withdrawn. By the second half of life, many women recognize that their nervous systems have been carrying the imprint of decades of adaptation.

This is not pathology. It is physiology.

For years, many women have lived in states of heightened alertness without naming it as such. Responsibility, caretaking, emotional labor, leadership, and achievement require vigilance. The nervous system adapts by remaining partially activated. This allows responsiveness, productivity, and endurance. It also prevents full rest.

Over time, this state becomes familiar.

The body learns to stay ready.

Rest becomes shallow. Presence becomes harder to access. Joy remains elusive. Muscles remain subtly tense. Breathing stays shallow even in moments of quiet. The body remains braced long after the original demands have passed.

The nervous system does not respond to logic alone.

It responds to experience.

This is why insight alone rarely produces lasting change. A woman may understand intellectually that she needs rest, boundaries, or honesty. But if her body has learned that safety is conditional – earned through performance, compliance, or vigilance – it will remain alert until it experiences something different.

This chapter is not about diagnosing trauma.

It is about recognizing adaptation.

Many women were not unsafe in obvious or dramatic ways. But they were required to be constantly responsive. They learned to anticipate others, manage emotional climates, prevent disruption, and carry responsibility quietly. The nervous system learned that regulation depended on control. That rest came only after everything else was handled. That composure was necessary and collapse was dangerous.

As women enter the second half of life, this strategy often stops working.

The body becomes less willing to maintain constant activation. Symptoms surface. Fatigue that does not resolve with sleep. Anxiety without a clear cause. Irritability that feels disproportionate. Emotional reactivity that surprises her.

These are not failures of resilience. They are messages.

The nervous system knows when a woman is living out of alignment.

## Safety Is the Organizing Principle

Safety is the central concept here. Not comfort. Not ease. Safety means the nervous system can downshift. It means the body does not expect harm, abandonment, or overload.

Many women are surprised to realize how rarely they feel truly safe – not physically, but internally.

Safety is created through consistency, honesty, and boundaries. When women stop forcing themselves into situations that require bracing, the nervous system begins to settle. When truth replaces performance, regulation becomes possible.

One woman described how her anxiety diminished only after she stopped agreeing to commitments that left her depleted. Another noticed that her body relaxed for the first time in years when she stopped managing her partner's emotions. These changes were not cognitive breakthroughs. They were physiological responses. The body responded before the mind fully understood what had shifted.

The nervous system also responds to rhythm.

Irregular schedules, constant stimulation, and unpredictable demands keep it on edge. When women establish rhythms that honor rest, transition, and presence, the nervous system recalibrates. This is why practices like walking, breathing, gentle movement, touch, and quiet are so effective. They speak the nervous system's language directly.

Connection plays a central role.

The nervous system is social. It regulates through relationship. When women feel seen without performing, heard without explaining, and accepted without earning, the body relaxes. This is why authenticity restores desire. Why boundaries deepen intimacy. Why shared power feels stabilizing rather than threatening.

Regulation does not mean constant calm. It means flexibility.

A regulated nervous system can mobilize when needed and settle afterward. Many women have lived in mobilization without recovery for decades. Learning to downshift is not weakness. It is intelligence.

As women age, nervous system capacity changes. Tolerance for overload decreases. Recovery takes longer. Sensitivity increases. This is not decline. It is information. The nervous system is refining what it will carry. It is asking for sustainability rather than endurance.

Understanding this reframes everything.

Rest is not laziness. It is regulation.

Boundaries are not selfish. They are stabilizing.

Desire is not unpredictable. It is responsive to safety.

Time feels scarce when the nervous system is activated and spacious when it is settled.

This is also why rushing often backfires. When women attempt to overhaul their lives quickly, the body resists. It interprets speed as threat. Change that honors the nervous system unfolds gradually. It builds capacity rather than overwhelming it.

This chapter is not about mastering the nervous system.

It is about listening to it.

The nervous system does not need to be controlled. It needs to be respected.

When women live in ways the nervous system

recognizes as safe, aligned, and sustainable, something profound happens. Energy returns. Clarity sharpens. Relationships feel less charged. Life becomes more livable.

The nervous system knows what the mind may still be debating.

It knows when a woman is living truthfully.

It knows when she is no longer available for patterns that deplete her.

And it responds with relief.

This intelligence has been present all along.

The second half of life offers an opportunity to finally trust it.

## Reflective Questions

1. How does your body signal safety or threat in everyday situations?

2. Where do you notice chronic bracing, tension, or vigilance in your life?

3. What roles or patterns have required you to stay constantly alert?

4. How do rest, boundaries, and honesty affect your sense of calm and clarity?

5. Where does your nervous system feel most settled and supported?

6. How does your experience of time change when your body relaxes?

7. What would it mean to trust your nervous system as a source of wisdom rather than something to override?

# CHAPTER 17:
# THE BODY AS ALLY

*"The body is where our story becomes honest."*

— Parker Palmer

I thought I had learned my lesson.

After surgery, after recovery, after writing about listening to the body, I believed I understood the language of limitation.

And then I went skiing in Vail with my family.

It was one of those luminous weeks, clear mountain air, the kind of blue sky that feels almost theatrical. My two sons, Michael and Tommy, were strong on the slopes. My six-year-old granddaughter, Maven, fearless and laughing, flew down the mountain as if gravity were a game she had already mastered.

Watching her filled me with joy. And something else.

A quiet insistence: *Keep up.*

At seventy-six, I strapped on my skis and followed. I told myself I would take it slowly. I told myself I would stay on manageable terrain.

But there is a subtle pride that accompanies capability. I have always been active. Always strong. Always able to participate.

My knees, however, had other data.

The downhill pressure. The repeated torque. The accumulated strain from decades of movement. My right knee, already carrying a meniscus tear from another ski trip years ago, began whispering.

A tightness.

A stiffness at night.

A slower rise from the lodge bench.

I minimized it.

"It's just soreness," I said. "We're all tired."

The following week, back in my home in Florida, I played golf with friends at Ocean Golf Course at The Breakers in Palm Beach. The ocean breeze was perfect. The fairways immaculate. I walked the course, swung the club, laughed with my friends between holes.

By evening, my knee felt heavy.

The next morning, it refused. I woke with sharp, immobilizing pain. When I tried to stand, my leg would not bear weight. The inflammation was visible. Angry. Unambiguous. I could not walk without assistance.

There is a specific shock in waking up and realizing your body has drawn a boundary you did not authorize.

Now, as I am writing this book, I sit with ice packs and anti-inflammatory medications. I test different strategies. I negotiate stairs carefully. I move more slowly than I want to.

And I ask myself the question that echoes through this entire book:

Why do I still override my body? Even now. Even after surgery. Even after writing about presence and attunement.

Is the desire to perform stronger than the discipline to observe boundaries?

I suspect the answer is not arrogance. It is identity.

I do not want to be the grandmother who sits in the lodge while others ski. I do not want to be the golfer who declines the back nine. I do not want to be the woman who says, "I can't."

Capability has been part of my self-concept for so long

that limitation feels like diminishment.

But here is what the knee is teaching me, and teaching me more persistently than theory ever could:

The body is not preventing participation. It is redefining it. It is asking a more refined question:

What is sustainable now?

At seventy-six, the spirit may still feel forty. The memory of strength remains vivid. But joints, cartilage, inflammation, these are not abstract. They are biological realities.

The body is not punishing me. It is protecting me from cumulative damage. It is asking me to recalibrate participation rather than abandon vitality.

Perhaps I ski half-days, I choose gentler runs. Perhaps I ride the lift down once and watch Maven with delight instead of competition.

Perhaps I play nine holes and leave while still strong.

The ally does not always say yes.

Sometimes it says enough.

And perhaps this is the deeper work of the second half of life:

To separate aliveness from overexertion.

To understand that vitality does not require self-violation.

To recognize that boundaries are not evidence of decline, but of intelligence.

The question is not whether we will face limitation. We will.

The question is whether we meet it with resentment or partnership.

My knee is not the enemy.

It is the messenger.

And I am still learning to listen.

## When the Body Interrupts Your Identity

There comes a moment, sometimes sudden, sometimes gradual, when the body interrupts the story you have been telling about yourself.

You have always been the strong one. The energetic one. The capable one. The one who keeps up.

Then something refuses.

A knee that won't cooperate.

A back that tightens.

A heart that races unexpectedly.

Fatigue that no longer yields to discipline.

And what hurts is not only the physical sensation. It is the identity disruption.

If I cannot do what I have always done, who am I now? This is where many of us become adversarial with our bodies. We push harder. We negotiate. We medicate without listening.

We compare ourselves to younger versions of ourselves.

But what if the interruption is not sabotage? What if it is refinement?

In the second half of life, the body often becomes more specific.

It no longer tolerates excess. It does not absorb strain as quietly. It demands pacing. This is not decline alone.

It is intelligence insisting on sustainability. When the body interrupts your identity, you are invited to ask:

- What part of my self-concept depends on performance?

- Where am I proving vitality instead of preserving it?

- Am I participating from joy – or from fear of being left behind?

- What would honoring this limitation make possible?

Limitation can feel humiliating.

But it can also be clarifying.

Perhaps you are not meant to ski the steepest run, but you are meant to watch your granddaughter with full presence instead of divided attention.

Perhaps you are not meant to play eighteen holes, but you are meant to leave the course energized rather than inflamed.

Perhaps the body is not removing you from life. It is repositioning you within it.

Aliveness is not measured by intensity. It is measured by coherence.

The body as ally does not promise that you can do everything you once did. It promises that if you listen early enough, you can continue participating wisely, sustainably, and without resentment.

When the body interrupts your identity, it is asking a gentler question than you may think:

Can you be whole without overexerting? The answer is not found in pushing. It is found in partnership.

By the second half of life, the body is no longer abstract. It can no longer be ignored, optimized indefinitely, or disciplined into compliance. It changes. It signals. It limits. And it remembers. These changes are often framed as loss, yet they also open the possibility of a different relationship, one rooted not in control, but in partnership.

To treat the body as an ally is not to deny its vulnerability. It is to recognize that the body remains intelligent and communicative, even when it no longer behaves as it once did. Strength may fluctuate. Energy may arrive unevenly. Recovery may take longer. These shifts do not make the body unreliable. They require a different form of listening.

Many women spend much of their lives managing their bodies rather than inhabiting them. The body becomes an instrument, something to maintain so that responsibilities can be met and life can proceed uninterrupted. In the second half of life, interruption becomes unavoidable. Health issues emerge. Sensations demand attention. Fatigue refuses to be negotiated away. The body insists on relationship.

At first, this insistence can feel like betrayal.

My friend Kate described it that way after her illness. She had always trusted her body to perform. She exercised, ate well, rested when she could and assumed resilience was something she could count on. When she became ill, it was not dramatic at first — just a growing heaviness, breathlessness she couldn't explain, an exhaustion that lingered. Then came the diagnosis, the treatments, the long months of recovery.

What surprised her most was not the physical limitation, but the emotional rupture.

"I felt like my body had turned against me," she said. "I had done everything right."

In the early months, she tried to reclaim control. Kate pushed herself to return to routines. She measured progress by how close she could get to her former capacity. Each setback felt personal. Each limitation felt like failure.

The shift came quietly.

One morning, instead of forcing herself through a walk she felt she *should* be able to do, she stopped. She sat on a bench and noticed her breath. She felt the sun on her face. She let her body set the pace rather than argue with it.

Nothing dramatic happened.

But something softened.

Over time, Kate listened differently. Fatigue was no longer an obstacle to overcome; it became a signal to slow down. Pain was not an enemy; it was a boundary.

The body was not withdrawing support — it was renegotiating terms.

This renegotiation required grief. She mourned what her body once allowed without question. She released assumptions about control, predictability, and fairness. These losses were real. They deserved acknowledgment, not forced optimism.

Yet alongside grief, something else emerged.

Kate's priorities clarified. Trivial concerns lost urgency. She became more selective — not only about how she spent her energy, but with whom. She noticed moments of pleasure she had once rushed past: the satisfaction of rest, the comfort of stillness, the intimacy of being fully present for small things.

Her body had not betrayed her.

It had redirected her.

Illness and physical change do not arrive with instruction manuals. They alter identity as much as routine. They require women to release old agreements – those based on endurance, override, and postponement – and enter into new ones grounded in responsiveness.

Even within limitations, the body continues to offer guidance. It signals when rest matters more than effort. When connection matters more than productivity. When presence sustains more than performance.

The body also carries memory. It remembers stress that was minimized, grief that was postponed, and joy that was fully embodied. When women begin listening differently, they often recognize how much the body has held silently. This recognition can be tender. It can also be relieving. The body has been present all along, even when it was ignored.

Mortality becomes more visible in this season. Friends grow ill. Partners age. Loss becomes personal rather than theoretical. The body's fragility mirrors life's finitude. This awareness does not necessarily diminish vitality. Often, it intensifies it. When life is no longer assumed, it is met more fully.

Treating the body as an ally does not require constant positivity or resignation. It asks for responsiveness without self-judgment. It invites adjustment without collapse. It means honoring limits without surrendering engagement.

The body does not demand withdrawal from life.

It asks for a different quality of presence.

This book has emphasized vitality, pleasure, rest, and agency. These remain available even alongside illness, caregiving, or physical change. Aliveness is not the absence of difficulty. It is the capacity to remain present within it.

Some readers may be navigating uncertainty, caregiving, or grief. Others may be living with chronic conditions or new diagnoses. These experiences do not exclude anyone from the life described here. They shape how it is lived. They refine what matters.

The body as ally asks for trust rather than domination. Curiosity rather than frustration. Collaboration with what is, rather than endless mourning for what is not.

In this season, the body becomes less something to conquer and more something to accompany. It offers truth, even when that truth is uncomfortable. It offers presence, even when certainty is gone.

The body does not promise endless strength. It offers honesty.

And in the second half of life, honesty may be one of the most faithful forms of support we have.

## Reflective Questions

1. How has your relationship with your body evolved across different stages of your life?

2. Where have physical changes or health challenges asked you to renegotiate how you live?

3. What signals does your body offer that you are still learning to trust?

4. How have experiences of illness, caregiving, or loss reshaped your priorities?

5. Where do you notice moments of aliveness even alongside limitation?

6. What would it mean to respond to your body with curiosity rather than frustration?

7. How might treating your body as an ally change the way you inhabit this season of life?

# CHAPTER 18:
# TIME RECLAIMED

*"The bad news is time flies.*
*The good news is you're the pilot."*

—— Michael Altshuler

Time was reclaimed for me not in a quiet morning of reflection, but in immobilization.

After skiing in Vail and playing golf the following week, my right knee decided the matter for me.

It was not subtle.

I woke unable to stand without sharp, immediate pain. The joint was inflamed, swollen, uncooperative. Each attempt to bear weight felt like negotiation with a boundary I could not override.

The first morning, I told myself it would improve by afternoon. By the second morning, it had not. I sat on the edge of the bed, phone in hand, scrolling through the week ahead. Meetings scheduled. Calls confirmed. Commitments made weeks earlier. Lunches arranged. A board discussion. A strategy session. Every entry assumed mobility. Every entry assumed availability.

For decades, I had structured my life around forward motion. My calendar was proof of contribution. Empty space had once made me uneasy.

Now, my body was immovable.

I hesitated before opening my email. Canceling two weeks of appointments felt dramatic. Irresponsible. Almost indulgent.

What if something important happened without me?

What if I missed an opportunity?

What if momentum slowed?

The old reflex stirred quickly.

Push through. Adjust. Show up anyway.

But I could not physically walk.

And so, with a steadiness that surprised me, I began typing.

"I need to reschedule."

"I'm temporarily unavailable."

"I'll reconnect in two weeks."

One by one, I cleared the calendar. As each confirmation of cancellation arrived, I expected resistance. Instead, I received kindness.

"Take care of yourself."

"We'll reconnect when you're ready."

"No problem at all."

No crisis.

No unraveling.

No urgent follow-up.

The world did not collapse.

No one missed me.

That realization landed gently but unmistakably.

For years, I had believed my presence was necessary to sustain momentum. That if I stepped away, even briefly, something would falter.

But nothing faltered.

In fact, something in me settled.

The first few days were uncomfortable. I moved slowly through my home, icing my knee, elevating it, watching the rhythm of the day pass without my intervention. I noticed how often I reached for my phone out of habit rather than need.

Without appointments to attend, I was left with something I had rarely permitted myself:

Time without assignment. At first, it felt like loss. Then it began to feel like restoration.

I read without skimming. I sat without multitasking. I allowed healing to occur without narrating productivity around it. And as the inflammation gradually reduced, another clarity surfaced. Many of my commitments were inherited from earlier seasons. Some still aligned. Others existed because I had once said yes reflexively and never revisited the agreement.

The knee had interrupted urgency.

And in doing so, it exposed how much of my busyness was habit rather than intention. Reclaiming time did not require retirement. It required interruption. The surprising truth was not that I needed rest. It was that the world did not require my constant availability. The perceived opportunities I feared missing were largely imagined. The value I believed I was protecting through presence was not diminished by absence.

For two weeks, my body dictated pace.

And instead of feeling irrelevant, I felt recalibrated. Time, I realized, is not reclaimed by force. It is reclaimed by boundary.

My knee was not only healing. It was teaching. That urgency is often self-imposed.

That availability is often overestimated. That stepping back does not erase impact.

In stillness, I found something unexpected. Not emptiness. Agency.

Time had not been lost.

It had been returned.

## "But I Can't Slow Down."

If you are reading this and thinking, *That's easy for you to say. I can't clear my calendar. I have responsibilities. Deadlines. People who depend on me*, I understand. Not every woman can cancel two weeks of appointments.

But time reclaimed does not always begin with subtraction. Sometimes it begins with tempo.

I am thinking of my friend Elena. Her life remained full. She ran a consulting practice. She cared for aging parents. She was involved in her grandchildren's lives. Her calendar did not empty.

But something changed in her interior pacing. Before, she moved through her days with an invisible clock always running slightly ahead of her. Even in conversation, she leaned forward mentally, anticipating the next task. After her health scare, less dramatic than surgery, but serious enough to alarm her, she made a quiet decision:

She would not reduce responsibility immediately. She would reduce reactivity. She began with mornings. Instead of reaching for her phone before her feet touched the floor, she waited ten minutes. Ten minutes of breath. Of looking out the window. Of allowing her nervous system to settle before absorbing the world's demands.

Her calendar remained full. But she entered it differently. In meetings, she stopped interrupting silence to accelerate resolution. She let others finish their thoughts. She responded instead of reacting.

When a problem arose, she paused before offering solutions. "Let me think about that," became a legitimate answer instead of an admission of weakness.

Her workload did not diminish overnight. Her internal velocity did. Elena stopped double-booking out of habit. She built fifteen-minute buffers between commitments, not to add more, but to absorb what had just occurred.

At first, she felt inefficient. Then she felt effective. Nothing in her external life collapsed. In fact, her decisions improved. Her communication sharpened. Her evenings became less mentally crowded. She did not reclaim time by having less to do. She reclaimed it by inhabiting what she was already doing. Slowing down is not always about removing commitments.

It is about removing compulsion. It is about noticing the reflex to rush, and declining it. You may not be able to cancel two weeks. But can you reclaim ten minutes before your day begins?

Can you allow one conversation to unfold without accelerating it? Can you say, "I'll get back to you," instead of responding instantly? Can you move from urgency to intention in even one area of your life?

Reclaiming time is less about volume. More about posture. You can live a full life at a sustainable pace. You can remain engaged without remaining frantic.

The knee forced my pause.

Elena chose hers.

Both **led** to the same insight:

Time is not only something we manage. It is something we embody. When you slow your internal clock, even slightly, you step back into the pilot's seat.

Not because the sky has cleared.

But because you have.

For much of life, time is experienced as something external, something that acts upon us rather than something we inhabit. It presses forward, accelerates, and demands **a** response. Days are organized around urgency. Weeks are measured by productivity. Years are evaluated by milestones reached or deferred. In this orientation, time is rarely felt as spacious. It is endured, managed, or chased.

Many women have lived expertly within this structure. They have learned how to optimize schedules, multitask efficiently, and move quickly from one demand to the next. This competence has enabled accomplishment and responsibility. It has also created a relationship with time that is shaped more by pressure than by presence.

By the second half of life, many women sense that this relationship no longer fits. The pace that once felt necessary now feels abrasive. Urgency lingers even when the original demands have eased. The body slows, but the internal clock continues to race. This mismatch creates a kind of exhaustion that rest alone does not resolve.

Urgency is learned.

It is absorbed through cultural messages that equate speed with relevance and productivity with worth. Many women have spent decades in environments where slowing down meant falling behind, losing value, or disappointing others. Even when external pressures recede, the internalized pace remains. Time continues to feel scarce, even when it is no longer objectively constrained.

Reclaiming time does not begin with calendars or boundaries. It begins with awareness. It asks: How is time being experienced internally? Does it feel rushed or spacious? Fragmented or continuous? Oppressive or companionable? These questions reveal whether a woman is living in relationship with time or in resistance to it.

Presence expands time.

When attention is scattered, moments collapse into **a** blur. Days pass quickly but feel thin. When attention is gathered, time opens. A single conversation fully inhabited can feel richer than an entire day spent multitasking. Presence does not add hours to the clock. It deepens experience.

Many women are surprised to discover how much time is consumed by anticipatory anxiety and retrospective rumination. The future is rehearsed repeatedly. The past is replayed and revised. The present becomes a narrow corridor between them. When women notice this pattern without judgment, something shifts. Time is reclaimed not by doing less, but by being where they are.

One woman described realizing that she was rushing through moments she had waited years to reach: quiet mornings, unstructured afternoons, evenings without obligation. The urgency she carried had outlived its purpose. When she allowed moments to complete themselves without filling them, time felt generous again.

## Time as Choice

Thinking of time as choice reframes this experience. Instead of asking how to fit more into limited hours, the question becomes: what deserves to be here?

This discernment is not about withdrawal or minimalism. It is about alignment. When time is chosen intentionally, even ordinary days feel coherent. Life begins to feel authored rather than reactive.

As women age, the illusion of endless time fades. This awareness can provoke anxiety or clarity. In that softening, discernment sharpens. Choices become cleaner. The life that remains is no longer measured by volume, but by coherence.

Living beyond urgency does not mean disengaging from life. It means refusing unnecessary haste. It means recognizing that speed is not a measure of significance. Some things require time to ripen. Conversations deepen when they are not rushed. Decisions clarify when they are not forced.

Time as companion offers a gentler posture. Time is no longer an adversary to outrun, but a medium through which life unfolds. When women stop fighting time, they often discover they have more of it – not in quantity, but in quality.

Spaciousness brings clarity.

When life is lived at a constant sprint, intuition is drowned out. Choices become reactive. Patterns remain invisible. In spaciousness, signals emerge. Priorities organize themselves. The nervous system settles enough to register what is true.

One woman shared that her greatest sense of freedom came not from having fewer obligations, but from releasing internal urgency. She still worked. She still contributed. What changed was how she moved. She paused more often. She listened longer. Time felt livable again.

Reclaiming time is also relational. When women stop rushing themselves, they stop rushing others. Conversations become less transactional. Presence replaces performance. Relationships deepen not because more time is spent, but because time is used differently.

This chapter does not argue against ambition or contribution. It argues for coherence. When time is lived rather than managed, life feels less fragmented. Effort becomes intentional. Rest becomes restorative. Joy becomes accessible without being scheduled.

Time reimagined is not endless. It is intentional. It honors finitude without panic. It allows a woman to live fully within the time she has, rather than constantly negotiating with the time she imagines she lacks.

In the second half of life, reclaiming time is not about slowing everything down. It is about aligning pace with truth. When women inhabit time differently, life becomes less about urgency and more about presence.

This is what it means to reclaim time. Not to control it, but to live inside it.

## Reflective Questions

1. How do you most often experience time, as pressure, obligation, or presence?

2. Where does urgency persist in your life even when it is no longer required?

3. How does your body signal when you are rushing internally?

4. What moments do you move through quickly that you once longed to reach?

5. How does presence alter your perception of time passing?

6. What becomes clearer when you allow more spaciousness into your days?

7. What would it mean to treat time as a companion rather than an adversary?

# CHAPTER 19:
# AGING WITHOUT APOLOGY, RELEASING SHAME AND TRUSTING YOURSELF

*"The privilege of a lifetime is to become who you truly are."*

— Carl Jung

For many women, aging carries an unspoken burden. It is not only the awareness of time passing or the body changing. It is the quiet pressure to soften, shrink, or recede without naming the loss this implies. From an early age, women are taught that value is tied to youth, agreeableness, and appeal. As these markers shift, many women internalize a sense of having passed their prime, even when their inner lives are richer, clearer, and more grounded than ever.

This is where apology begins.

It rarely arrives as a single thought. It shows up subtly. In how a woman speaks about her age with qualifiers or humor that diminishes. In how she minimizes her experience to avoid seeming out of step. In how she hesitates to claim authority without explanation. The apology is often silent, carried in tone, posture, and self-expectation rather than words.

Aging without apology begins internally. It requires recognizing how deeply shame has been absorbed. Shame for no longer being new. Shame for needing rest. Shame for having opinions, boundaries, or desires. This shame is not the result of personal failure. It is cultural inheritance.

Many women notice that as they age, their tolerance for pretense diminishes. They become less willing to perform optimism, attractiveness, or agreeableness to maintain comfort around them. They speak more plainly. They choose more selectively. This shift often brings relief and fear at the same time. Relief because the effort of self-editing lessens. Fear because stepping out of apology can feel like social risk.

Aging without apology does not mean rejecting grief. Many women grieve aspects of aging honestly. Physical changes. Reduced stamina. Shifts in visibility. The loss of ease that once felt automatic. Aging without apology allows grief without self-rejection. It acknowledges loss without turning it into diminishment.

Releasing shame requires self-trust.

In earlier life, external feedback often guided decisions. Approval, advancement, and recognition provided orientation. In the second half of life, these signals become less reliable. They may arrive less frequently or feel less relevant. Self-trust replaces them. This trust is not bravado or certainty. It is the steadiness that no longer rushes to defend itself.

Women who trust themselves are less reactive to judgment. They are not immune to it, but they are less governed by it. They know what they have endured. They know what they have learned. They no longer feel compelled to audition for legitimacy.

One woman described how she stopped correcting people when they underestimated her. She no longer rushed to prove relevance or competence. She allowed silence to do the work. What she discovered was not erasure, but discernment. She became more selective about where she invested energy. Her life grew quieter, but more truthful.

Trusting oneself also means accepting limits without moral judgment. Energy fluctuates. Capacity changes. Recovery takes longer. Priorities narrow. These are not signs of decline. They are signs of refinement. The body and psyche are clarifying what matters and what no longer needs to be carried.

Aging without apology is not about confidence as performance. It is about alignment. When a woman is aligned, she does not need to defend her presence. She inhabits it. Her authority is not loud. It is steady. It is felt.

This chapter invites an inner reckoning. Where has apology become habit rather than choice? Where have cultural messages been internalized without question? Where might self-trust replace self-correction?

Aging without apology does not require confrontation. It requires clarity. It allows a woman to stand inside her life without shrinking it for others' comfort. It replaces self-monitoring with self-respect. The end of apology is not arrogance.

It is peace.

## Reflective Questions

1. Where do you notice yourself minimizing, qualifying, or apologizing for your age?

2. What messages about aging did you absorb earlier in life that no longer feel true?

3. How has your relationship with self-trust evolved across different stages of your life?

4. What forms of shame still surface around visibility, desire, or authority?

5. How do you respond internally to physical or energetic changes as they arise?

6. Where might acceptance replace self-judgment in this season of your life?

7.  What would it mean to trust the woman you are
    now more than the woman you once were?

# CHAPTER 20:
# VOICE, VISIBILITY, AND BEAUTY REDEFINED

*"It takes courage to grow up and
become who you really are."*

— E. E. Cummings

A few days ago, I stood in front of the mirror and did not immediately adjust.

No repositioning the light.

No turning slightly to the side.

No scanning for what needed improvement.

Just standing.

The bathroom was quiet. Early light filtered in through the window, soft enough to be kind but honest enough to reveal everything. I saw the lines around my eyes more clearly than I once did. The softness at my jaw. The subtle settling of skin along my arms. A body shaped by seventy-six years of living.

For decades, the mirror had been a place of evaluation.

Is it holding up?

Does it still measure?

Can it still compete?

I had not consciously framed it that way, but the

orientation was there – beauty as maintenance, beauty as currency, beauty as subtle permission to remain visible.

But that morning, something shifted.

Instead of correcting, I observed.

I noticed how I stood, upright, steady. I noticed the way my shoulders rested naturally instead of pulled back to appear firmer. I noticed the rhythm of my breath.

This body had carried children. Negotiated boardrooms. Walked hospital corridors.

Skied mountains, even when it protested. Sat beside bedsides through grief.

Played golf under the Florida sun. It had endured surgeries. It had healed. It had adapted.

The lines I once tried to soften were the evidence of laughter and intensity. The softness was not neglect; it was biology. The changes were not failure; they were chronology.

For the first time in a long time, I felt at home. Nothing about my appearance changed that morning. My relationship with it did.

Beauty, I realized, had been something I pursued as permission, permission to feel relevant, permission to feel seen, permission to enter rooms without apology.

But what if beauty in the second half of life is not about permission at all?

What if it is about coherence? Coherence between how I feel and how I present. Between comfort and expression. Between vitality and truth.

I began dressing differently, not dramatically, but intentionally. Clothes that felt aligned with my body rather than contoured to disguise it. Shoes that supported movement instead of signaling endurance. Fabrics that moved with me rather than constricted me.

Not to attract attention. Not to withdraw from it. But to inhabit myself without negotiation. This is not resignation. It is embodiment. Resignation says, *It no longer matters*. Embodiment says, *It matters differently.*

Beauty in youth often performs. Beauty in maturity resonates.

It is less about symmetry.

More about steadiness.

Less about surface.

More about presence.

A woman at ease with herself radiates something unmistakable. It is not flirtation. It is not strategy. It is not demand. It is groundedness. And groundedness is magnetic.

Redefining beauty, for me, meant this:

Beauty is the visible expression of self-trust. It is the way you walk into a room without bracing. The way you sit without tightening. The way you meet your reflection without argument.

The second half of life does not remove beauty. It removes performance.

What remains is truer.

And truer, I have learned, is far more compelling.

Once the internal apology loosens, something else becomes possible: expression that matches inner truth.

Aging without apology is not only an internal posture. It reshapes how a woman moves through the world, how she speaks, how she occupies space, how visible she allows herself to be. The inner shift toward self-trust naturally seeks an outer form. What has been quietly reorganizing within begins to show.

For many women, voice has been carefully managed across decades. They learned when to speak, how much to say, and how to soften truth so it would be received. They learned to qualify opinions, to offer reassurance before conviction, and to place harmony above clarity. These adaptations were often necessary. They protected relationships and created opportunity. Over time, however, they became habits rather than choices.

Aging can intensify this silence. Cultural narratives suggest that older women should recede gracefully, speak less forcefully, and make room for others. Yet many women experience the opposite impulse. As experience accumulates, clarity increases. As self-trust deepens, the desire to speak honestly strengthens. What once felt risky now feels necessary.

Voice returns when permission is granted internally.

This does not mean speaking more often or more loudly. It means speaking without self-erasure. When a woman stops apologizing for her presence, her words carry weight. They are not rushed. They are not hedged. They arrive from lived experience rather than approval-seeking. Silence becomes an ally rather than a threat. Pauses are allowed. Words land.

My friend Ana described how she stopped qualifying her expertise in professional settings. She no longer prefaced insight with disclaimers or self-effacing humor. The response was immediate. She was listened to differently – not because she demanded authority, but because she no longer apologized for it.

Visibility undergoes a similar transformation.

For some women, invisibility arrives uninvited with age. They are interrupted less, consulted less, or overlooked entirely. For others, invisibility becomes a refuge – a relief from the scrutiny and performance of earlier years. Aging without apology restores choice. A woman may choose visibility on her terms. She may decide when and where to be seen, and when privacy feels more nourishing. Both are expressions of agency.

Visibility without apology is not about reclaiming youth or attention. It is about claiming presence. It allows a woman to be seen as she is now – not as she was, and not as she is expected to be. This presence is quieter, but more grounded. Less reactive. More intentional.

Another Rita shared how she allowed herself to be seen creatively later in life, after years of postponement. She did not seek validation. She simply shared what felt true. The relief came not from recognition, but from expression itself. Visibility became an act of integrity rather than performance.

Beauty, too, is redefined in this season.

For much of life, beauty is treated as a form of currency. It is cultivated, evaluated, compared, and exchanged for approval or belonging. It is shaped by external standards that rarely evolve as women do. Aging exposes the fragility of these standards. What once promised value no longer fits lived reality.

At first, this can feel like loss.

But many women discover something unexpected: when beauty is no longer pursued as permission, it becomes presence.

Beauty in the second half of life becomes less about surface appeal and more about coherence. A woman who is at ease with herself radiates a different kind of presence. It is not performative or strategic. It is grounded. It is felt.

Many women describe dressing differently, not to attract attention, but to feel aligned. Choosing comfort without apology. Expression without explanation. Movement without display.

This is not resignation.

It is embodiment.

Beauty becomes visible in posture, voice, and ease. In how a woman inhabits a room. In how she listens without shrinking. In how she allows her body to take up space without negotiation. Beauty shifts from something to achieve to something to inhabit.

This redefinition can unsettle others.

A woman who speaks clearly, occupies space, and no longer performs youth challenges familiar expectations. Some may interpret this as arrogance or defiance. It is neither. It is integrity. The discomfort it provokes is not hers to manage. It is a natural response to change.

Aging without apology externally is not about visibility for its own sake. It is about congruence. When inner truth is allowed to take outer form, life feels less fragmented. Voice, body, and presence align.

This chapter affirms something essential: Voice is not aggression. Visibility is not vanity. Beauty is not currency. They are expressions of selfhood. They belong to women at every stage of life.

When women allow themselves to be visible without apology, they contribute something the world needs deeply: perspective shaped by time, depth shaped by experience, and presence shaped by self-trust. They remind the world that growth does not stop with youth. It deepens.

Aging without apology is not defiance.

It is arrival.

## Reflective Questions

1. How has your voice changed over time, and where have you learned to soften or silence it?

2. In what spaces do you feel most visible, and where do you choose to hide?

3. How do you define beauty now, separate from cultural or youthful standards?

4. What fears arise when you imagine being fully seen at this stage of life?

5. How does your body express confidence, hesitation, or alignment?

6. Where might visibility feel nourishing rather than draining?

7. What would it mean to occupy space without apology, simply as yourself?

# CHAPTER 21:
# THE WISDOM OF TIMING

*"There is a time for everything, and a season
for every activity under the heavens."*

— Ecclesiastes 3:1

What surprised me most was not the technology. It was the relief. When I first began exploring AI, I expected to feel behind. Overwhelmed. Perhaps even irrelevant in a world accelerating faster than any generation before mine.

Instead, I felt oriented. There was no scramble. No desperate attempt to catch up. No performance of fluency. Just curiosity.

For years, I had believed that timing was external, that opportunity belonged to the young, the fast, the early adopters. That if you did not enter at the beginning, you entered too late.

But as I sat learning something entirely new, I realized something unexpected: I was not late. I was prepared.

Decades of experience, pattern recognition, discernment, synthesis allowed me to approach new tools without intimidation. I did not need to prove mastery. I did not need to mimic youth. I could integrate what was useful and discard what was noise.

It was not about technology. It was about alignment.

There is a distinct feeling when something arrives at the right moment in your life.

It does not feel frantic. It does not feel competitive. It does not require reinvention of identity. It feels like expansion. The body softens instead of bracing. Curiosity rises instead of comparison. Energy increases rather than drains.

In earlier seasons, I might have rushed toward something new to stay relevant. Or avoided it out of fear of inadequacy. This time, I simply entered. The difference was not competence.

It was timing.

Wisdom of timing is the ability to recognize when you are no longer acting from insecurity or proving, but from readiness. There are opportunities that would have overwhelmed you ten years ago. There are roles you were not mature enough to hold five years ago. There are conversations you could not have navigated earlier without defensiveness. And there are seasons when waiting is not procrastination – it is preparation.

We often interpret delay as failure. But sometimes delay is gestation. The right moment carries a different texture.

You do not force it. You do not chase it. You recognize it.

Learning AI was simply the catalyst that revealed this truth to me: I was not chasing relevance. I was participating in evolution. Not to compete. But to contribute.

The second half of life offers a unique advantage. You are less desperate. Less impressionable. Less driven by comparison.

When something new appears, you can ask calmly: Is this aligned with who I am now? If the answer is yes, you enter.

If the answer is no, you decline without panic. Timing is not about speed.

It is about coherence. And coherence has its own

clock.

## How to Recognize Your Right Moment

The right moment rarely announces itself loudly. It does not arrive with fireworks. It does not demand immediate action. It does not create panic. In fact, it feels surprisingly calm. Here are a few ways to recognize it:

### 1. Your Body Is Curious, Not Contracted

When something is mistimed, the body tightens. The breath shortens. You feel pressure to decide quickly. There is urgency in the nervous system.

When the timing is right, curiosity replaces tension. You lean in rather than brace. The idea energizes you instead of depleting you.

### 2. You Are Not Trying to Prove Anything

If you are pursuing something to outrun irrelevance, impress someone, or repair insecurity, the timing may be reactive.

When the moment is right, you are not proving. You are expanding. The action feels like alignment, not compensation.

### 3. The Decision Feels Clean

Right timing carries a kind of internal simplicity. Even if the path ahead is challenging, the yes feels uncluttered. You do not need elaborate justification.

There may still be risk, but not chaos.

### 4. You Can Walk Away Without Collapse

If the opportunity disappeared tomorrow and you would feel devastated or diminished, you may be attaching identity to it.

When timing is wise, you choose freely. If it unfolds, good. If it does not, you remain whole.

### *5. It Builds From Who You Already Are*

The right moment does not require becoming someone entirely different. It builds naturally from your lived experience. It integrates your past rather than abandoning it.

The wisdom of timing is less about prediction and more about attunement.

You do not chase the moment.

You recognize it.

## How Aging Sharpens the Instinct of Timing

Youth often equates speed with relevance. Move quickly. Decide early. Enter first. Do not miss out. There is energy in that season, and sometimes it serves you well. But maturity introduces something more powerful than speed: Discernment.

With age comes pattern recognition. You have seen cycles rise and fall. Trends surge and dissolve. You know that urgency is often manufactured. You understand that not every open door must be walked through.

Time teaches pacing.

In earlier decades, I may have pursued new ventures out of fear of being left behind. I may have said yes before fully understanding the cost. I may have mistaken opportunity for obligation.

Now, something steadier governs my choices. I can feel when something aligns with my deeper arc. I can sense when a conversation is premature. I can tolerate waiting without interpreting it as failure.

Aging sharpens the instinct of timing because it reduces panic. You are less seduced by comparison. Less threatened by others' momentum. Less dependent on applause. You know that seasons exist. You have lived through reinvention before.

And perhaps most importantly, you understand that not every chapter must be maximal to be meaningful. There is a quiet confidence in choosing later. In entering when you are ready, not when the world is loudest. In saying no without defensiveness. In trusting that the right moment does not require desperation. Maturity does not slow relevance. It refines it. The wisdom of timing is not about doing less. It is about doing what is yours, at the moment it is truly yours to do. And that instinct, like so much in the second half of life, grows stronger when you stop racing the clock and start listening to it.

One of the quiet advantages of the second half of life is a transformed relationship with timing.

After years of responding quickly, pushing forward, and equating movement with progress, many women sense something subtler. Wisdom does not always arrive through action. Sometimes it arrives through restraint. Sometimes through waiting. Sometimes through the clear recognition that a chapter has already completed itself.

Timing is not indecision. It is discernment.

Earlier in life, speed is often rewarded. Initiative is praised. Momentum is encouraged – even when clarity is incomplete. Many women learn to act first and integrate later, trusting that competence and effort will compensate for uncertainty. This builds resilience and capability. It also teaches women to override intuition in favor of responsiveness.

In the second half of life, intuition often becomes more trustworthy.

Patterns have repeated often enough to be recognized. Consequences are easier to anticipate. The cost of misaligned action is clearer. The body signals readiness or resistance more distinctly. Timing becomes something felt rather than calculated.

One woman described reaching a crossroads she had been preparing for at least on paper for years.

It promised recognition.

But her body disagreed.

Instead of excitement, she felt dull heaviness. Not fear, but more like reluctance. Her mind argued with the sensation. She told herself she was being overly cautious, that hesitation meant she was losing confidence, and that waiting might mean missing her moment.

She almost said yes. What stopped her was not clarity, but the discomfort of forcing it.

At first, waiting felt unbearable. She questioned herself daily. She worried she was confusing wisdom with avoidance. She watched others move quickly and wondered if she was falling behind. The urge to act did not disappear; it pulsed.

Waiting was not peaceful. It was active restraint. Weeks passed. Then months passed. During that time, new information surfaced. Conversations revealed complexities that had been invisible at first. The opportunity itself shifted.

Most importantly, her internal state changed. What had felt heavy became clear, not because the opportunity improved, but because her resistance sharpened. She realized she didn't want the role she was being offered. She wanted what she hoped it would give her. When she finally declined, she felt something unexpected: relief. Not relief from pressure alone, but also relief from self-betrayal avoided.

Nothing immediately replaced what she released. There was space. Uncertainty. A period of not knowing. And yet, she described that time as grounded rather than anxious. Her energy stabilized. Her attention widened. When the next opportunity appeared, one she could not have predicted, it arrived without urgency. Her yes felt clean. This is one face of the wisdom of timing. But timing is not only about waiting. It is also about recognizing when *now* truly is the moment.

One of my clients, Ruth, described feeling uneasy, not because she was being pushed too quickly, but because she sensed she was waiting too long. She had been hearing about artificial intelligence everywhere. At first, she dismissed it as something for younger people, technical professionals, or future consideration. She told herself she would learn it "later," once it became clearer, more stable, or more necessary.

But instead of calm, she felt increasing tension. She noticed a subtle anxiety when conversations turned to AI. A sense of being left out. A growing awareness that decisions were being shaped by tools she didn't understand. Her hesitation was not grounded. It was defensive. The difference mattered.

When she paused to listen more closely, she realized her body wasn't signaling *yet*. It was signaling *pay attention*. She began slowly. No urgency. No pressure to master anything.

She signed up for a short introductory workshop and took notes by hand. She opened the platform in the quiet morning before emails began to accumulate. She asked it simple questions first, how to summarize an article, how to outline an idea she had been circling for months. She experimented with drafting a paragraph and then rewriting it in her voice. She noticed where it helped and where it fell flat.

She learned what AI was, and what it wasn't.

She explored how it could support creativity, organization, research, and problem-solving, not as a replacement for her judgment, but as an extension of it. When a suggestion felt misaligned, she discarded it. When a prompt sparked clarity, she followed it. The relationship was collaborative, not dependent. There was no rush to become an expert. There was only curiosity.

This is the other expression of the wisdom of timing. Knowing when to act is just as important as knowing when to wait.

AI represents one of those inflection points where waiting too long carries a cost, not of irrelevance, but of unnecessary dependence. This moment invites learning, not mastery. Engagement, not perfection. Curiosity, not performance.

In the second half of life, timing becomes less about chasing every opportunity and more about recognizing which ones reshape the landscape. AI is not a passing trend. It is a structural shift in how work, creativity, learning, and decision-making are supported.

For women with experience, discernment, and context, this is not a threat. It is leverage.

The wisdom of timing asks different questions than ambition once did: Not *can I do this*, but *is this the moment*. Not *will this make me impressive*, but *will this keep me oriented and sovereign*.

Waiting is wisdom when it protects alignment. Action is wisdom when it prevents erosion.

The body often knows timing before the mind agrees.

Heaviness signals misalignment.

Restlessness signals readiness. Anticipation signals arrival.

These sensations are not guarantees. They are guidance.

As women age, urgency often diminishes – not because desire fades, but because discernment sharpens. There is less appetite for forcing outcomes and more tolerance for allowing life to meet them halfway. This does not weaken agency. It refines it.

The wisdom of timing also includes knowing when not to act at all.

Not every impulse requires execution. Not every opportunity deserves pursuit.

Selectivity protects energy and preserves meaning.

This chapter is not an argument for passivity. It is an argument for precision. Action taken at the right time feels different. It carries less resistance. It requires less justification. It does not demand constant reassurance. It feels clean. In a culture that prizes immediacy, honoring timing can feel countercultural. Yet it is often what separates effort from effectiveness. When women trust timing, they stop confusing speed with progress and activity with purpose.

The second half of life offers fewer illusions about control. What remains is the opportunity to act with integrity, to wait without anxiety, to let go without bitterness, and to move when the moment is ripe rather than when pressure demands it.

Timing does not promise certainty. It offers coherence. Learning to trust timing is learning to trust oneself. Sometimes wisdom arrives as *not yet*. Sometimes as *now*. Sometimes as *no longer*.

And once that difference is felt in the body, it becomes one of the most reliable guides a woman has, not only for action, but for peace.

## Reflective Questions

1. How has your relationship with timing changed over the course of your life?

2. Where have you acted too quickly – and where have you waited too long?

3. What does your body signal when waiting is wise versus when action is needed?

4. Where might learning something new now – such as AI – support your independence and clarity?

5. How do you distinguish between fear-based hesitation and grounded restraint?

6. What are you holding onto past its natural season?

7. What would it mean to trust timing as an expression of self-trust rather than delay?

# CHAPTER 22:
# LIVING WITH ENOUGH

*"Enough is a feast."*

d— Buddhist Proverb

The numbers did not require checking. I knew that. The accounts were stable. The investments diversified. The reserves more than adequate for the season of life I was in. And yet, late at night, I opened the banking app anyway.

Just to look. I scrolled through balances. Reviewed recent transactions. Verified transfers that had already been confirmed. I ran quiet mental calculations I had run dozens of times before.

Nothing had changed. Still, I felt a flicker of relief when the screen reflected what I already knew: We are fine. The relief lasted minutes.

Then the subtle tension returned. Scarcity thinking does not always come from actual lack. Sometimes it comes from memory. From early seasons of building, stretching, negotiating, calculating every decision carefully. From decades of responsibility. From knowing what it takes to create security, and fearing, however irrationally, how quickly it could disappear.

I told myself I was being prudent. Responsible. Strategic. But if I am honest, the late-night checking was not strategy. It was anxiety disguised as vigilance.

The same pattern appeared in other places. I said yes to projects I did not need. Joined boards I did not have time for. Filled calendar space quickly, as if empty hours might evaporate if left unclaimed.

I accumulated commitments the way some people accumulate possessions, not from greed, but from fear of running out.

Running out of relevance.

Running out of opportunity.

Running out of purpose.

It is remarkable how easily a woman who has achieved "enough" can continue living as if she is one decision away from insufficiency. Scarcity is not only financial. It is psychological.

I remember one particular afternoon when I was reviewing an investment opportunity that, objectively, I did not need. The return was modest. The risk manageable. It was a reasonable decision.

But the urgency I felt was disproportionate. "If I don't move now, I'll miss it," I thought.

Miss what?

Security I already had?

Validation of being active?

The comfort of motion?

I paused. And in that pause, I recognized something uncomfortable: I was not investing from abundance. I was reacting from habit. For decades, forward motion equaled safety. Growth equaled protection. Accumulation equaled control.

But in this season, the numbers were not the issue. My internal posture was. Living with enough requires more courage than striving for more. Because enough removes the distraction of pursuit. It forces you to confront the deeper question:

If I am already secure, who am I without urgency?

Scarcity thinking whispers that you must keep going,

keep acquiring, keep proving, keep saying yes, because stopping invites vulnerability.

But what if stopping invites clarity?

That evening, instead of making the investment immediately, I closed the laptop. I did not decide from pressure. I decided to wait. The waiting felt almost rebellious. And in that small act of restraint, something shifted.

Enough is not a number. It is a stance.

It is the decision to believe that what you have, financially, relationally, experientially, does not require constant reinforcement to remain valid. Living with enough does not mean withdrawing from growth. It means refusing to operate from fear when fear is no longer necessary. The scarcity that once fueled survival can quietly outlive its usefulness. And unless you examine it, it will continue running your life long after you have outgrown it.

For much of life, enough feels perpetually out of reach. There is always another milestone to achieve, another improvement to make, another expectation waiting just beyond the horizon. Satisfaction becomes conditional. It appears briefly and fades as the next goal emerges. Desire becomes shaped by comparison, and worth is measured against moving targets. Enough is experienced briefly, if at all, before urgency returns.

By the second half of life, many women question this orientation. They notice how quickly accomplishments lose their impact, how effort expands to fill every available space, how scarcity persists even in the presence of abundance. This awareness does not arrive as self-reproach. It arrives as fatigue. A deep, embodied knowing that something essential has been postponed for too long.

Living with enough is not about settling, resignation, or lowering standards. It is about recognizing sufficiency when it is present and allowing it to register. It is a shift in attention rather than circumstance – a willingness to let what is already here count.

Scarcity is often internalized long before it is material. Many women carry a constant background sense that there is not enough time, not enough security, not enough appreciation, not enough margin. This posture fuels responsibility, vigilance, and endurance. It also erodes ease. Even when external needs are met, the internal stance remains braced, scanning for what might go wrong or what still needs fixing.

Sufficiency begins internally. It emerges when a woman pauses long enough to acknowledge what is stable, supportive, and sustaining without immediately searching for what is missing. This acknowledgment can feel unfamiliar, even uncomfortable. Scarcity has momentum; it keeps the nervous system alert. Enough invites rest.

One woman described realizing that she had been living as if something essential were always just beyond reach. When she stopped and named what was already steady in her life – her relationships, her resources, her capacity – she felt a surprising mix of relief and grief. Relief at recognizing what had been holding her all along. Grief for how long she had lived without allowing herself to feel the steadiness beneath her.

Living with enough does not eliminate desire. It transforms it. Desire becomes less frantic and more discerning. Instead of reaching indiscriminately, it clarifies what matters. This clarity reduces excess effort and increases satisfaction. Wanting becomes intentional rather than compensatory.

Sufficiency also reshapes how women relate to accumulation. Many find they want fewer things, fewer commitments, fewer obligations. This is not withdrawal from life. It is refinement. Energy is no longer scattered; it is gathered. Attention becomes more focused. Choices feel cleaner.

There is courage in claiming enough. In a culture that equates more with success, enough can be misinterpreted as complacency. Yet it takes strength to stop striving when striving is no longer necessary. It takes trust to believe that worth does not diminish when accumulation slows. Claiming enough is not giving up. It is arriving.

Enough also alters how women relate to others. Comparison loses its grip. Competition softens. Generosity increases. When a woman is no longer operating from scarcity, she does not need to measure herself against others to feel legitimate. She can appreciate difference without threat and success without envy.

This chapter is not an argument against ambition or growth. It is an invitation to let growth emerge from fullness rather than lack. When enough is acknowledged, growth becomes organic instead of compulsive. Expansion arises from curiosity and alignment rather than fear of falling behind.

Many women discover that living with enough does not shrink their lives. It expands them. Time feels more spacious. Relationships feel less transactional. Joy becomes more accessible because it is no longer postponed until everything is resolved or perfected.

Sufficiency also offers resilience. When life inevitably changes, when losses occur, when resources fluctuate, the internal anchor of enough remains. It provides steadiness that does not depend on constant reinforcement. Enough becomes a reference point rather than a reward.

Living with enough does not mean that everything is resolved. It means that what is unresolved no longer dominates attention. It allows a woman to live in proportion, responding to challenges without losing sight of what is stable and sustaining.

Enough is not a destination. It is a practice. It requires returning again and again to the present moment and asking a simple question: what is here now that supports me? Over time, this question becomes easier to answer. The nervous system relaxes. Gratitude becomes less forced. Presence deepens.

In the second half of life, living with enough is an act

of wisdom. It honors effort without being owned by it. It allows gratitude without denial. It creates room for joy that does not need to be justified or earned.

Enough is not the absence of desire.

It is the presence of sufficiency.

## Reflective Questions

1. Where in your life do you still operate from a sense of scarcity rather than sufficiency?

2. What does enough feel like in your body when you allow yourself to experience it?

3. How has comparison shaped your sense of satisfaction over time?

4. What becomes possible when you stop postponing contentment?

5. Where might claiming enough feel risky, unfamiliar, or undeserved?

6. How does acknowledging sufficiency change your relationship with desire and ambition?

7. What would it mean to trust that what you have right now is enough to begin from?

# CHAPTER 23:
# MENTORSHIP WITHOUT CONTROL

*"The task of the mature adult is to hold
authority without insisting on obedience."*

— Parker Palmer

For over ten years, I led the organization. It was not just a title. It was history. Relationships. Institutional memory. Donor dynamics. Political nuance. Quiet alliances that had taken years to build. I knew which conversations required delicacy. Which board members needed advance preparation. Which traditions mattered more than they appeared.

When it became time to transition, I did not step away casually. I chose her carefully.

She was intelligent, capable, ambitious in the right way. She had energy I recognized, the kind I once carried in earlier seasons. I believed in her.

The mentoring process lasted over a year. We met regularly; I walked her through our nonprofit organization's mission and vision, not just our mission-based programs but the personalities behind them. I shared past mistakes. Explained tensions that were not documented in any file.

Introduced her personally to key stakeholders so the relationships would feel relational, not procedural.

I brought her into meetings where I intentionally let her speak first. When board members looked to me for confirmation, I redirected them gently. "She's leading this now," I would say. It was not symbolic. It was strategic. I wanted her to feel authority before I exited.

The final months required discipline. I resisted the urge to correct small decisions. I allowed her to handle minor missteps without stepping in to smooth them. I understood that leadership confidence is not inherited; it is earned through experience.

The official transition was graceful. A farewell gathering. Kind words. A formal handoff. I left believing the relationship would evolve into collegiality.

Perhaps occasional calls. Shared reflection. Mutual respect across seasons. Instead, there was silence. At first, I told myself she was busy. The early months of leadership are consuming. There are fires to manage. Visibility to establish.

Weeks passed. Then months. No update. No thank-you note beyond the public remarks. No private acknowledgment of what had been transferred. I noticed the absence before I named it.

I would hear of organizational developments through others. Decisions made. Directions chosen. My name gradually removed from communication threads.

It was appropriate. It was also jarring. The silence lasted longer than I expected, nearly a year before any personal outreach occurred, and even then it was brief, professional, contained.

There was no hostility. Just distance. And, if I am honest, it hurt. Not because I needed praise. But because I had imagined continuity.

I had poured knowledge, access, credibility, and care into her preparation. I had stepped aside deliberately so she could stand fully. I had relinquished control without sabotage.

And in return, there was... absence. This is the unspoken risk of mentorship. You give without contractual return. You prepare someone to outgrow you. You invest in their authority, knowing that once they claim it, they may not circle back.

In the early months of that silence, I felt the subtle tug of ego.

*Did I matter?*

*Was the work appreciated?*

*Was I naïve to expect acknowledgment?*

But gradually, something steadier surfaced. I had mentored her to lead. Not to remain connected to me. Authority without control means releasing not only the role, but the outcome. It means accepting that your influence may not be named publicly. It means trusting that what you transferred will show up in ways you may never witness.

The silence was not necessarily rejection. It was differentiation. She needed to establish her leadership without orbiting mine. And maturity required that I not interpret her autonomy as ingratitude.

Mentorship without control is not sentimental. It is disciplined. You give fully. You step back completely. And you do not insist on loyalty as repayment.

That is harder than it sounds.

But it is the difference between guidance and possession.

For a time, I wondered what it meant.

Was she simply overwhelmed by responsibility?

Was gratitude postponed or unexpressed?

Was something unspoken pressing quietly against the surface?

Eventually, I realized the questions themselves were no longer useful.

Mentorship is not a contract. It is an offering.

Whatever her reasons, I know this: I did my very best. I showed up with integrity. I gave what I had to give. And that is enough. The satisfaction did not come from recognition or return. It came from knowing I had made a difference in another soul's life. Having mentored someone thoughtfully, fully, and without expectation was complete in itself.

This is where mentorship in the second half of life often begins. By this stage, influence arrives whether it is sought or not. Experience accumulates quietly. Perspective deepens through living rather than striving. Others notice. Younger women look not only for answers but for examples.

With this influence comes a subtle tension.

How does one offer guidance without overreaching?

How does one share wisdom without imposing it?

How does one remain relevant without clinging to authority?

Mentorship without control begins with restraint.

Earlier in life, influence is often tied to responsibility. Decisions feel urgent. Outcomes matter. Direction seems necessary. Many women have spent decades managing consequences, smoothing paths, and protecting others from error. These habits are understandable. They are often praised. But they do not automatically loosen when circumstances change. Control can persist long after it has ceased to be helpful.

In this season, mentorship shifts from directing to witnessing. The goal is no longer to shape outcomes, but to support discernment. This requires trust – both in the other person's capacity to learn and in one's own ability to step back without disappearing.

Letting go of control does not mean withholding insight. It means offering perspective without attachment to whether it is taken. Advice becomes an invitation rather than a prescription. Wisdom is shared without urgency. The mentor's role is not to convince, but to illuminate.

This sounds elegant in theory. In practice, it can be costly.

Restraint is not always rewarded with appreciation, continuity, or loyalty. Sometimes mentorship ends in silence. Sometimes it asks the mentor to release not only authority but recognition. This does not diminish the value of what was given. It clarifies it.

Many women feel the discomfort of watching others make choices they themselves would not make. This discomfort is instructive. It often reveals where control has been mistaken for care. True mentorship allows for difference. It honors learning that happens through lived experience rather than protection. Growth that is earned carries a different kind of authority.

This does not mean mentors should tolerate harm or abandon boundaries. There are moments when intervention is necessary. But many situations live in the gray space between responsibility and autonomy, where restraint feels risky precisely because it is motivated by love.

Mentorship without control requires humility.

It acknowledges that one's own path, while instructive, is not universal. Context matters. Temperament matters. Each woman's desires matter. Now, the ownership is clear and parallel. When women release the unconscious hope that others will validate their choices by replicating them, mentorship becomes more spacious and more honest.

There is also relief in this shift.

Carrying responsibility for others' outcomes is exhausting. When control is released, relationships soften. Trust deepens. Influence grows quieter and more enduring.

One woman described how her relationship with her adult daughter changed when she stopped offering solutions unless asked. Conversations grew less defensive. Her daughter shared more openly. Guidance emerged naturally rather than being resisted. The bond strengthened not through instruction, but through respect.

Another noticed how younger colleagues responded when feedback was framed as reflection rather than directive. Instead of compliance, she received engagement.

Instead of distance, she experienced genuine respect. Authority held lightly proved more powerful than authority asserted.

Mentorship without control recognizes that growth is not linear. People must encounter their edges. They must test limits. They must make mistakes and learn from them. The mentor's role is not to prevent this process, but to remain available without judgment.

This chapter also speaks to legacy. Contribution often shifts from building to transmitting. What is passed on is not only knowledge, but posture. How one holds power teaches more than what one says.

When women model boundaries, self-trust, and restraint, they teach these qualities implicitly. When they resist the urge to manage others' lives, they demonstrate confidence in the unfolding of life itself. This confidence is deeply reassuring to those still finding their way.

Mentorship without control does not diminish relevance. It deepens it.

Influence that is not forced is more likely to endure. Wisdom that is offered freely is more likely to be received. And contribution that is given without expectation is complete the moment it is offered.

The greatest gift many women offer is not direction, but steadiness. Not answers, but perspective. Not control, but trust.

This is mentorship rooted in maturity. It honors autonomy while remaining connected. It allows others to grow without being supervised. And it asks the mentor to find satisfaction not in outcomes or gratitude, but in the quiet knowledge that a life was touched.

And that, on its own, is alignment.

## Reflective Questions

1. When have you offered guidance without receiving acknowledgment, and how did you make meaning of that experience?

2.  Where in your life do you still feel responsible for others' outcomes?

3.  How has control been confused with care in your relationships?

4.  What wisdom do you carry that can be offered freely, without attachment to its use?

5.  Where might restraint deepen trust rather than diminish influence?

6.  How do you remain present when you cannot resolve another person's choices?

7.  What would mentorship look like if making a difference – rather than being remembered – were enough?

# CHAPTER 24:
# THE FEMININE AS
# STABILIZER

*"The feminine does not rush, it steadies."*

— Maria L. Ellis

In times of acceleration, instability, and fragmentation, restoration rarely comes through more force. It comes through containment. Through rhythm. Through presence. The feminine, not as gender, but as orientation, carries these qualities naturally. It is not limited to women, nor owned by them. It is a way of relating, attentive, integrative, responsive, available to anyone willing to embody it.

When embodied rather than idealized, it becomes one of the most stabilizing forces available to families, organizations, and cultures under strain.

Much of modern life has been shaped by speed. Output is rewarded. Urgency is normalized. Decisiveness is prized over discernment. Many women learned to survive and succeed within these systems by adapting to their values. They developed strength through endurance, responsiveness, and control. These capacities were necessary. They were also incomplete.

Systems optimized solely for efficiency eventually lose

resilience.

When pace outstrips integration, instability grows quietly beneath the surface. Burnout increases. Relationships thin. Decision-making becomes reactive. What is missing is not competence, but coherence.

The feminine offers a different kind of intelligence.

It attends to context rather than abstraction.

It notices impact rather than intention.

It values continuity over conquest.

Sustainability over speed.

This intelligence is not soft. It is integrative. It can hold complexity without collapsing into it. It stabilizes not by dominating uncertainty, but by remaining present within it.

Throughout this book, we have explored how women reclaim rest, desire, time, sufficiency, authority, and trust in the body. These are not personal indulgences. They are stabilizing contributions. A regulated nervous system affects everyone in its field. A woman who inhabits time differently reduces urgency around her. A leader who mentors without control creates trust instead of compliance.

Stability emerges not through instruction, but through embodiment. It reconnects what has been separated – body and mind, effort and meaning, power and care. This is not sentimental work. It is structural. It changes how systems function simply by changing the quality of presence within them.

One woman described how her leadership shifted when she stopped forcing outcomes and began attending to relational dynamics. She noticed how quickly meetings moved past unresolved tension. Instead of pushing decisions through, she slowed the process just enough for listening to occur. Meetings lengthened slightly. Conversations deepened. Resistance softened. Decisions improved. Burnout decreased. She was not doing less. She was stabilizing the system.

Another noticed how her family changed when she stopped managing everyone's emotions. She no longer anticipated conflict or absorbed tension preemptively. She regulated herself instead. At first, discomfort surfaced. Then responsibility redistributed. Others stepped forward. Stability emerged not through control, but through coherence.

But the stabilizing force of the feminine is not limited to households or teams. In the early months of the COVID-19 pandemic in 2020, public health agencies across the world faced extraordinary strain. Data shifted daily. Infection models were revised repeatedly. Hospitals filled. Citizens looked to leadership for clarity while scientists were still learning in real time.

In one national public health agency, like many others, daily press briefings became the central stage of crisis management. The pressure was immense.

Media demanded certainty. Politicians demanded solutions. The public demanded reassurance. Epidemiologists revised projections as new information emerged. Guidance around masks, school closures, and public gatherings evolved week by week.

In the early phase, leadership responded with speed and authority. Directives were issued rapidly in an effort to project control over uncertainty. Communication became increasingly declarative, firm, decisive, sometimes defensive.

The intention was stability. The effect, at times, was fragmentation. When policies changed, as they inevitably had to, trust eroded. When communication felt hardened rather than human, fear intensified. When complexity was reduced to certainty too quickly, later revisions felt like reversals rather than refinements.

Speed without relational grounding amplified anxiety.

Months later, as leadership dynamics shifted within certain institutions, a different tone emerged. The change was not dramatic or theatrical. It was subtle but perceptible.

Press briefings slowed. Phrases such as, "This is what we know today," and, "We are continuing to learn," appeared more frequently. The language acknowledged uncertainty rather than denying it. Experts were allowed to explain nuance instead of compressing conclusions into soundbites.

The posture softened without becoming weak. The stabilizing effect did not come from controlling the crisis. It came from containing it. The feminine stabilizing force does not eliminate chaos. It metabolizes it. It creates psychological safety not by pretending certainty, but by holding complexity without panic. It tolerates ambiguity long enough for truth to mature. It resists the reflex to overpromise in order to appear strong.

In times of institutional crisis, this energy is often misunderstood. It may look slower.

It may sound less absolute. It may frustrate those who crave immediate clarity. But steadiness is not the same as slowness. And acknowledgment of uncertainty is not weakness.

The feminine stabilizer at the cultural level does three essential things:

1. It regulates tone before issuing directives.
2. It prioritizes relational trust alongside factual accuracy.
3. It communicates evolution as learning, not reversal.

This is not about gender. It is about energy.

Men embody this stabilizing force. Women embody it. Institutions can cultivate it, or suppress it. In crisis, command-and-control leadership may produce short-term order. But long-term cohesion requires something deeper: the capacity to remain grounded while the environment destabilizes.

We saw this not only in national agencies but in hospitals, school districts, and local governments. Leaders who admitted what they did not know, while remaining present and responsive, often built greater trust than those who projected certainty prematurely. The feminine as stabilizer does not seek to dominate the storm. It seeks to steady those inside it.

In the second half of life, many women discover this quality within themselves more consciously. They no longer rush to appear decisive. They allow complexity to breathe. They hold authority without escalating volume.

What we witnessed during that global crisis was not simply policy in motion. It was leadership temperament under pressure. And temperament, more than speed, determines whether a system fragments or coheres.

When leadership shifted, the approach changed. The new leader did not promise certainty. She did not accelerate decision-making to appear decisive. Instead, she slowed communication, spoke carefully, and named uncertainty without dramatizing it. She prioritized consistency over novelty, coordination over reaction, and transparency over reassurance. Information was released in rhythm rather than bursts. Listening preceded policy. Presence replaced posturing.

Public anxiety decreased, not because the crisis resolved, but because the system felt held. Trust stabilized not through force, but through containment. This is the feminine at work on a cultural scale.

The feminine stabilizes by holding space rather than filling it. It allows tension without rushing to resolution. It trusts process. It recognizes that not all problems require immediate action. Some require attention, patience, and integration.

Importantly, the feminine does not belong exclusively to women. It is a human capacity. Women, however, have often been its primary carriers, particularly in systems that neglect it. For much of history, this stabilization happened quietly, without recognition.

In the second half of life, many women stop compensating silently and begin stabilizing visibly.

This visibility matters.

When feminine intelligence remains unseen, it is undervalued. When it is embodied openly, it reshapes norms. It legitimizes pacing, listening, and care as strengths rather than liabilities. It challenges the assumption that leadership must be urgent to be effective.

Culturally, this orientation is increasingly necessary.

Periods of rapid change strain systems. When speed outpaces integration, collapse follows. The feminine counters this pattern by insisting on embodiment, relationship, and rhythm. It restores balance where fragmentation dominates.

This chapter is not a call for women to carry more responsibility. It is an acknowledgment of what naturally occurs when women live aligned. Stabilization emerges as a byproduct of coherence. It does not require self-sacrifice. It requires self-trust.

The second half of life often supports this alignment. Performance loosens. Authenticity strengthens. Presence deepens. What results is not withdrawal, but a different form of contribution, one that steadies rather than accelerates.

The feminine stabilizer does not dominate. It grounds.

It does not accelerate. It steadies.

It does not fragment. It integrates.

As this book moves toward its conclusion, this chapter widens the lens. The personal transformations described here ripple outward. They influence how women lead, parent, partner, mentor, and participate in culture itself.

And the feminine, when honored, embodied, and visible, offers exactly that.

## Reflective Questions

1. Where have you noticed your presence naturally calming or stabilizing others?

2. How have you embodied feminine intelligence without naming or claiming it?

3. Where have systems around you benefited from pacing, listening, or integration?

4. How do you distinguish stabilization from control in your life?

5. Where might your lived alignment be a contribution beyond the personal?

6. How does honoring the feminine change how you relate to power and authority?

7. What would it mean to value steadiness as a form of impact?

# CHAPTER 25:
# WHERE YOU BEGIN

*"Start where you are. Use what you have. Do what you can."*

— Arthur Ashe

Many women reach the end of this book feeling something shift internally, while their external circumstances remain unchanged.

Clarity has arrived. Life has not paused.

Responsibilities persist. Meetings are still scheduled. Family members still call. The inbox still fills.

And so the question emerges quietly: If I see more clearly now, where do I begin?

Let me tell you about my friend, Lila. She did not leave her job. She did not end her marriage. She did not move cities or make announcements.

She began on a Tuesday.

## The First Week

Lila was a partner in a small firm. Two adult children. A mother whose health required periodic attention. A marriage that was steady, if slightly tired. Her calendar was layered and predictable.

After finishing this book, she did not make a list. She noticed.

That first week, she began paying attention to her internal reactions.

On Wednesday, during a meeting, she heard herself agree to lead a new initiative before she had fully assessed her capacity. She felt the familiar tightening in her chest, the reflexive "yes" that had served her for years.

This time, she paused.

"Let me check my current commitments before confirming," she said instead. The room did not collapse. She went home unsettled. Part of her feared she had appeared less capable. But something steadier whispered: *You told the truth.*

That was her first experiment. Not rebellion. Accuracy.

## The First Month

Over the next few weeks, Lila did not subtract major responsibilities.

She adjusted tempo. She built fifteen minutes of buffer between meetings so she could finish one before entering the next. She stopped answering non-urgent emails after 8 p.m. She told her husband, gently, that she no longer wanted to host every holiday gathering.

"I'm not withdrawing," she clarified. "I'm recalibrating."

He blinked, surprised. "Okay," he said slowly. "What would that look like?"

That question changed more than any argument would have. For the first time in years, she described what she actually wanted: fewer performative obligations, more intimate gatherings, time to write in the early mornings before the house stirred.

Nothing dramatic shifted. But resentment decreased. The small contradictions, where her outward compliance had masked inward resistance, began dissolving.

## The First Season

Three months later, Lila's life looked largely the same.

She still worked. She still cared for her mother. She still attended school events and professional commitments. But internally, she was inhabiting her life differently.

She said no without apology when something felt misaligned. She allowed silence in conversations rather than smoothing discomfort. She dressed in a way that felt like herself instead of what she believed was expected.

One afternoon, her daughter remarked, "You seem calmer." Lila smiled.

"I'm just not arguing with myself as much." That was the real shift. Choosing yourself is rarely about subtraction first. It is about reducing self-contradiction.

You begin by noticing where your words and your body disagree. You begin by telling smaller truths. You begin by experimenting inside your existing life rather than waiting for a cleaner stage.

The first week may bring discomfort. The first month may bring subtle recalibration. The first season brings evidence: nothing catastrophic happens when you stop over-functioning. Where you begin is not with exit. It is with honesty. And honesty does not require crisis. It requires courage, practiced in increments.

You do not need to dismantle your life to live it more fully. You need only to stop betraying yourself inside it. That is enough for a beginning.

Choosing yourself is not an event. It is not a declaration or a dramatic pivot. For most women, it begins as a series of small experiments that allow truth to surface without forcing outcomes before they are ready.

You do not begin by leaving everything. You begin by listening differently.

## Beginning Inside a Full Life

Many women postpone change because their lives feel too full to accommodate it. Careers are active. Families rely on them. Health requires attention. Financial and relational commitments are real. The idea that choosing yourself requires radical subtraction can feel impractical or even irresponsible.

It does not.

In fact, the most sustainable changes begin while life is still full. This is how discernment is tested in real conditions rather than ideal ones. Choosing yourself does not require withdrawing from responsibility. It requires withdrawing from unnecessary self-contradiction – saying yes while resentment gathers, agreeing outwardly while dissent grows quietly within.

The first question is not, What should I change? It is, Where am I already overriding myself?

Often, the earliest signals appear in small moments. The yes that feels heavy. The conversation that leaves you depleted. The habit of rushing that no longer serves you.

Noticing is the first act of choice.

## The First Week: Creating a Pocket of Space

In the first week of choosing yourself more consciously, nothing needs to change outwardly. This week is about attention, not action.

You might begin by noticing when your body tightens and when it softens. You might observe which obligations feel clean and which feel negotiated against yourself. You might pay attention to how often you apologize unnecessarily, explain preemptively, or rush to meet expectations before they are voiced.

This is not a week for decisions. It is a week for information.

One woman described this phase as simply pausing before responding. She did not change her answers yet. She just stopped answering immediately. That pause alone altered her nervous system. It reminded her that she had choice, even when she ultimately chose the same action.

Space does not need to be large to be meaningful. It needs to be intentional.

## The First Month: Running Small Experiments

The second phase often arrives as curiosity. What would happen if I tried this differently?

Rather than making sweeping changes, this is a season for experiments. Experiments are powerful because they reduce fear. They are temporary. They are informative. They do not demand permanence.

You might experiment with saying no to one nonessential obligation. You might choose one relationship where you stop over-functioning and see what happens. You might protect one morning a week from unnecessary noise or stimulation. You might rest without earning it and notice the internal response.

The goal is not success. It is feedback.

Some experiments will feel relieving. Others will feel uncomfortable. Both are valuable. Relief often signals alignment. Discomfort often signals an old pattern losing its grip. A behavior that once protected you but now constrains you.

Neither requires immediate interpretation.

During this month, many women discover that not everything needs to be decided now. Clarity emerges through lived response rather than intellectual planning.

## The First Season: Allowing Reorganization

Over a longer season, something subtler begins to happen. Life starts to reorganize itself around your steadiness.

When you stop rushing, others adjust. When you stop explaining, boundaries clarify. When you stop absorbing emotional labor automatically, responsibility redistributes. This does not happen instantly, and it does not happen without friction. But it happens more reliably than most women expect.

This season often includes grief. Grief for what no longer fits. Grief for relationships that cannot adjust. Grief for versions of yourself built for survival, not sustainability.

This grief is not a sign that you are doing something

wrong. It is a sign that something real is changing.

At the same time, new forms of support often emerge. Conversations deepen. Energy returns in unexpected ways. Life begins to feel less managed and more inhabited.

You do not need to orchestrate this process. You need to stay honest inside it.

## When Not to Act

One of the most important insights in this season is learning when not to act.

Not every realization requires immediate execution. Not every truth needs to be announced. Sometimes the most self-honoring choice is to wait until your nervous system is settled enough to move cleanly.

Waiting is not avoidance when it is conscious. It is integration.

You will know the difference by how your body feels. Action taken from alignment feels steady. Action taken from pressure feels urgent and brittle. Trust that distinction.

## You Are Not Late

Many women fear they are starting too late. That the time for change has passed. That choosing themselves now is indulgent or impractical.

It is not.

The second half of life is not a consolation prize. It is a season of precision. Fewer illusions. Clearer signals. Deeper capacity for truth. What you begin now is not a correction of the past. It is a refinement of how you live from here.

You do not need to have the whole path mapped. You need only to take the next aligned step.

This chapter is not an instruction manual. It is a reassurance. You do not need to blow up your life to live it more truthfully. You need to stop abandoning yourself in small, habitual ways.

Begin there.

## Reflective Questions

1. Where in your daily life do you most often override your needs or signals?

2. What small pause or boundary could you experiment with this week without creating disruption?

3. Which obligations feel essential, and which feel maintained primarily out of habit or guilt?

4. What does your body tell you when something feels aligned versus when it feels forced?

5. What would a small, reversible experiment in choosing yourself look like this month?

6. Where might waiting and listening serve you better than immediate action right now?

7. How would your life feel if you trusted that change could unfold gradually rather than all at once?

# CHAPTER 26:
# THE QUIET REVOLUTION

*"Some revolutions arrive without noise.*
*They change everything anyway."*

— Maria L. Ellis

Elena had always been the dependable one. For decades, she was the woman others called when something needed stabilizing. She chaired committees, hosted gatherings, organized fundraisers, managed family logistics, remembered birthdays, and anticipated tensions before they surfaced. Her competence was admired, and her reliability was unquestioned. She carried responsibility so seamlessly that few people stopped to consider how much weight she held.

Nothing dramatic marked the beginning of her change. There was no illness, no betrayal, no announcement of reinvention. Her life remained outwardly steady. What shifted was subtle and almost imperceptible at first.

One afternoon during a meeting, someone suggested she take on a new initiative because, as they put it, "You're always so good at these things." For years, her reflex would have been immediate agreement. Saying yes had been a form of efficiency, and perhaps also identity. This time, however, she paused long enough to notice the familiar tightening in her chest. Instead of agreeing automatically, she said calmly, "I don't think I'm the right person for that right now."

The room adjusted. No one argued. No one objected. But there was a small recalibration in the air. Elena did not offer elaborate explanations or apologies. She simply allowed her decision to stand.

In conversations, she began allowing silence to exist without rushing to fill it. Where she once would have softened awkward pauses or clarified every ambiguous remark, she waited. She listened more fully. She permitted others to carry their thoughts to completion. At first, people seemed slightly unsettled by the change. A colleague later told her that he wondered whether she was upset about something.

"I'm not upset," she replied evenly. "I'm just not rushing anymore."

At home, the shift continued. She stopped volunteering for tasks before anyone asked. She no longer assumed responsibility for orchestrating every holiday gathering. When her adult children called with dilemmas, she listened attentively but did not immediately offer solutions. Instead of absorbing their anxiety and converting it into strategy, she asked questions and trusted them to decide.

"You seem different," one of them observed.

"I'm learning to be," she said with a gentle smile.

Elena began resting without apology. She declined invitations when she felt tired without manufacturing elaborate excuses. She took afternoons to herself without framing them as productivity disguised as leisure. She read without multitasking. She walked without calculating steps. She allowed her energy to guide her decisions instead of overriding it.

Those around her sensed the change even when they could not name it. For years, Elena had been the emotional stabilizer in many rooms. She had absorbed tension before it escalated and managed dynamics before they became visible. Without her immediate smoothing, conversations sometimes lingered longer. Discomfort was not instantly resolved. Others were required to step forward in ways they had not before.

At first, this created subtle unease. Her predictability had been part of the structure others relied upon. When she stopped performing competence on demand, the ecosystem shifted.

Yet over time, something else emerged. Interactions with her became calmer. Decisions slowed slightly and improved. Because she spoke less frequently, her words carried greater weight. People listened more carefully when she did speak. Her presence felt grounded rather than reactive.

Elena was not doing less because she was exhausted. She was doing less because she was finished proving.

That distinction transformed her life.

The quiet revolution is not loud or theatrical. It does not require departure or confrontation. It begins internally, in the decision to withdraw energy from what requires performance and redirect it toward what invites presence. It is the choice to participate without over-functioning, to contribute without over-identifying, and to remain engaged without entanglement.

Elena did not shrink. Her life did not contract. In many ways, it became simpler without becoming smaller. She remained committed to her relationships and responsibilities, but she no longer carried more than was hers to carry. The steadiness she had once provided through effort now emerged through coherence.

Because when a woman stops performing, others are invited to stop performing as well. When she no longer rushes to stabilize every situation, those around her develop their capacity for steadiness. What once depended on her management begins to rest on shared maturity.

The quiet revolution is not rebellion. It is regulation. It is not withdrawal from life but alignment within it. It does not announce itself with declarations. It reveals itself through composure.

And in its composure, it changes the room.

Revolutions are often imagined as loud. They disrupt systems, challenge authority, and announce themselves through conflict and spectacle. History has conditioned us to expect rupture when meaningful change occurs. Yet the revolutions that endure rarely arrive this way. They begin quietly. They unfold internally. They do not overturn structures first. They reorient the people living within them.

This book has traced that kind of revolution. It is not a revolution that demands recognition, nor one that replaces ambition with withdrawal. It is a revolution that replaces proving with alignment. It does not reject the life you have lived. It refines how you now inhabit what remains.

This revolution does not arrive through a single decision or defining moment. It arrives gradually. It takes shape through noticing, through small refusals to abandon oneself, through choosing differently again and again until the internal center of gravity shifts. It arrives when a woman realizes that she no longer needs to justify her presence through effort.

Across these chapters, you have explored grief after success, receiving instead of achieving, intimacy without performance, rest as intelligence, time reclaimed, and the feminine as stabilizer.

These were not separate insights. They were expressions of the same movement toward coherence.

The quiet revolution begins when a woman stops organizing her life around external approval. She stops asking how she is perceived and begins asking whether she is aligned. This shift is subtle. It rarely provokes comment. Yet it changes every decision that follows.

Alignment simplifies life.

Internal negotiation softens. Choices feel cleaner. Boundaries require less explanation. When truth rather than expectation becomes the guide, effort becomes precise instead of exhausting. Presence deepens because energy is no longer scattered across competing demands.

In this revolution, success is no longer required to justify existence. Achievement may continue, but it no longer carries identity on its back. Contribution becomes an expression of coherence rather than hunger. A woman may still lead, create, build, and mentor, but these actions arise from clarity rather than compulsion.

Urgency loosens its grip. Time is no longer chased. It is inhabited. The nervous system settles into rhythms that sustain rather than extract. Rest ceases to be a reward and becomes a condition for discernment. Life begins to feel inhabitable again.

This understanding of inhabiting the present moment echoes a principle I explored more fully in *The Consciousness Blueprint*. Presence is not a discipline to master or a performance to maintain. It is a state of internal permission. When a woman is no longer divided against herself, presence arises naturally. It does not require constant vigilance. It requires alignment.

The quiet revolution also reshapes relationships. Love becomes less transactional. Intimacy becomes safer. Mentorship becomes generous rather than directive. Influence is exercised without control. Authority is held without force. Power circulates rather than concentrates.

This revolution is not performative. It does not seek validation or consensus. Many women will never name it. Others will sense it without understanding why. A woman living in alignment alters the emotional climate around her simply by being regulated, present, and self-trusting.

The final season is not defined by age or by proximity to the end of life. It is defined by completion. It is the season in which a woman stops preparing for life and begins inhabiting it fully. Earlier seasons are shaped by becoming, by building identity, capacity, credibility, and security. The final season is shaped by integration. What has been learned no longer needs to be proven. What has been earned no longer needs to be defended.

This does not mean doing less for the sake of reduction. It means doing what is essential. It means allowing truth to determine pace. It means releasing roles that once mattered but no longer fit. It means trusting discernment over urgency.

The quiet revolution asks for courage. It asks for the courage to rest without justification. It asks for the courage to speak without hedging. It asks for the courage to let timing, rather than fear, lead.

It also asks for patience. Alignment does not arrive fully formed. It is reinforced through daily choices rather than singular breakthroughs. There is no finish line. There is only increasing coherence.

Culturally, this matters more than it may appear. Systems shaped by speed, domination, and extraction are inherently unstable. Women living aligned lives offer a counterforce. They stabilize without preaching. They demonstrate sufficiency without argument. They model restraint, presence, and integration simply by how they live.

This is why the revolution is quiet. It does not need permission. It does not require agreement. It spreads through example.

As this book closes, there is nothing left to add. There is no directive to follow and no identity to assume. What remains is an invitation to trust what you already know.

You are not behind. You are not late. You are not diminished. You are in a season where alignment matters more than acceleration.

The quiet revolution does not promise ease. It promises truth. Truth, lived consistently, is one of the most stabilizing forces available.

This is not the end of becoming. It is the end of unnecessary striving.

What follows is presence.

Coherence.

A life that fits.

## Reflective Questions

1. Where in your life have you already begun this quiet revolution, even if you did not have language for it at the time?

2. What forms of proving, explaining, or performing are you now ready to release?

3. How does alignment feel different from effort in your body and nervous system?

4. Where has urgency softened as truth has clarified in your life?

5. How has your definition of success changed as you have moved through this book?

6. What would it mean to trust the season you are in without defending or explaining it to others?

7. How might your way of living quietly influence those around you without intention or force?

# CHAPTER 27:
# LEGACY, JOY, ABUNDANCE, AND WHAT WE LEAVE BEHIND

*"Legacy is not what we leave to people,
but what we leave in them."*

— Peter Strople

Legacy is often described in terms of what survives us: assets, titles, institutions, or accomplishments etched into history. Yet in lived experience, legacy is far more intimate. It is shaped in everyday moments: how we treat people when no one is keeping score. Long after achievements fade into the background, what endures is how people felt in our presence, and what they learned about life by watching how we lived.

After success, the question of legacy evolves. It becomes less about *What did I build?* and more about *What did I pass on?* Success provides resources, leverage, and influence. Legacy asks us to use those gifts to leave behind joy, wisdom, and abundance – not only financial abundance, but emotional security, ethical grounding, and a sense of possibility for future generations.

This theme has guided much of my writing. In *Family Business Legacy Plan*, I explored how wealth, leadership, and values can be transferred across generations without fracturing relationships or identity. In *Achieve Financial Freedom*, I focused on the practical foundations that allow individuals and families to move from scarcity-driven decisions to intentional, empowered living.

Together, these works reflect a central truth: money is a tool, not the legacy itself. What we teach others to do with that tool – how we hold it, steward it, and align it with our values – is what truly endures.

## Redefining Abundance Beyond Wealth

For many who achieve success, abundance initially means safety – having enough so worry can finally quiet down. Over time, a deeper realization often emerges abundance is not only what we accumulate, but what we normalize.

I have worked with families who did everything "right" financially – sound investments, careful estate planning, well-structured trusts – yet still sensed something missing. Their children were protected, but hesitant. Secure, but without direction. In these moments, the work shifted from spreadsheets to storytelling. When parents began sharing not just their wins, but their mistakes, fears, and turning points, something changed. The next generation didn't inherit anxiety; they inherited confidence. They learned that abundance includes resilience, adaptability, and trust in one's own judgment.

This insight echoes a core message from *Achieve Financial Freedom*: true freedom is not simply the absence of financial pressure, but the presence of choice. When future generations understand that money is meant to support life, not replace it, they are better prepared to use wealth wisely rather than fearfully.

## Joy as an Inheritance

Joy does not automatically follow success. In fact, many high achievers carry forward the same intensity that once drove results, even when it no longer serves them – or those watching them. Children and successors absorb not only what we say about life, but how we inhabit it.

I remember a moment with my family that clarified this for me. There was work to finish, responsibilities to manage, and deadlines pressing in. Yet I chose to pause – to laugh, to linger, to be fully present. Nothing extraordinary happened, and that was the point.

Joy does not need an occasion. It needs permission.

That permission becomes legacy. When future generations observe that success can coexist with laughter, rest, and connection, they internalize a healthier model of achievement – one that allows them to live fully rather than endlessly perform.

## Teaching without Lectures

The most enduring lessons are rarely delivered as advice. They are transmitted through example. Children, colleagues, and family members learn how to handle disappointment by watching how we treat ourselves after failure. They learn about integrity by observing whether our actions align with our stated values. They learn about abundance by seeing whether we share generously or cling tightly when we have more money than we truly need.

In *Family Business Legacy Plan*, I wrote about the dangers of transferring control instead of values. One leader I worked with realized that while his children respected his competence, they did not feel invited into his inner world. He changed course, not by giving instructions, but by sharing decisions he struggled with, ethical lines he refused to cross, and mistakes he wished he had handled differently. The lesson his children absorbed was not about business mechanics. It was about accountability, humility, and character.

## Leaving Foundations, Not Blueprints

A meaningful legacy does not require future generations to replicate our path. Their world will demand different skills, choices, and responses. When legacy becomes prescriptive, it can quietly turn into pressure.

Healthy legacy provides a foundation, not a script. It passes along principles that adapt responsibility rather than rigidity, curiosity rather than certainty, stewardship rather than entitlement. These ideas were central to *Family Business Legacy Plan*, where the emphasis was not on preserving exact structures, but on preserving purpose.

Leaving space for others to define success on their terms is one of the most generous acts of leadership available to us.

## The Emotional Ledger

Every family and organization carries an emotional ledger. It records whether love was expressed, whether apologies were offered, and whether mistakes were acknowledged or ignored.

Some of the most transformative legacy moments I have witnessed involved a simple sentence: "There are things I didn't do well, and I'm still learning." Those words do not diminish authority. They humanize it. They teach future generations that growth does not end with success; it deepens.

Clearing the emotional ledger often matters more than perfect planning. Without it, even well-designed financial legacies can feel heavy. With it, relationships remain intact and resilient.

## Legacy as a Daily Practice

Legacy is not something we leave behind at the end of life. It is something we practice daily. Each choice, to listen rather than correct, to rest rather than push, to share rather than hoard, quietly shapes the inheritance we are creating.

When legacy includes joy, it lightens the road ahead.

When it includes abundance, it reassures those who follow that there is enough, enough opportunity, enough love, enough room to become who they are meant to be.

In this way, legacy becomes less about being remembered and more about being felt, long after our voices fade, but while our values continue to walk forward through the lives of others.

## Reflective Questions

1. What do people consistently feel after spending time with me, and what does that suggest about the legacy I am living now?

2. How do I model joy, rest, and presence in a way others can give themselves permission to do the same?

3. What unspoken beliefs about money, success, or worth might others be absorbing from my behavior?

4. Which principles – not outcomes – do I most want future generations to carry forward?

5. Where might I be holding too tightly to control, identity, or expectations?

6. What conversations, acknowledgments, or apologies would meaningfully clear the emotional ledger?

7. What small, daily practices could better align my lived behavior with the legacy I hope to leave?

# BONUS CHAPTER: LIVING IN COHERENCE: *A SIGNATURE CLOSING PASSAGE*

*"Coherence is not something you achieve.*
*It is what remains when you stop contradicting yourself."*

— Maria L. Ellis

At the beginning of this book, we named a quiet truth many women recognize but rarely articulate: that competence can continue long after resonance has faded. That life can appear successful while feeling internally fragmented. That effort alone, no matter how disciplined or sincere, eventually stops working.

This insight did not arise in isolation. It echoes questions I explored earlier in my writing, particularly in *The Consciousness Blueprint*, where presence is described not as a practice to perfect, but as a state that emerges when internal conflict subsides. This book brings that principle fully into lived experience.

This bonus chapter returns to that truth, not to restate it, but to resolve it.

What most women are seeking in the second half of

life is not reinvention, healing, or optimization. It is coherence.

Coherence is the state when your inner life and outer life are no longer negotiating with each other. When what you value, what you choose, how you spend your time, and how your body responds begin moving in the same direction. It is the end of persuading yourself to tolerate what no longer fits.

Coherence does not arrive loudly. It often arrives as relief.

## When Life Stops Arguing with Itself

For much of life, self-contradiction is normalized. Women learn to override their bodies, soften their truth, manage emotional climates, and postpone rest in service of responsibility. These adaptations are not mistakes. They are intelligent responses to earlier demands. They are explored in depth in my longevity work, where endurance is honored for what it made possible but questioned for what it costs when carried too long.

One woman described coherence as the morning she realized she no longer needed to convince herself to show up. For years, her internal dialogue had been an argument. You should go. You can handle this. It will be fine once you get there. That morning, there was no argument. She simply moved.

Nothing dramatic had changed.
Her calendar looked the same.
Her responsibilities remained.
What changed was internal.

She had quietly stopped agreeing to commitments that required self-erasure, and over time, her nervous system stopped bracing. Showing up no longer required persuasion. That was coherence.

## The Body as the Final Arbiter

Throughout this book, and throughout my longevity

writings, the body has appeared again and again not as a problem to manage, but as a source of truth. Coherence is where that truth becomes unmistakable.

In *Designing Your Longevity*, I write about the body as a diagnostic instrument rather than an obstacle. One woman embodied this principle after years of low-grade anxiety that never escalated into crisis but never fully resolved. She exercised, ate well, practiced mindfulness, and could articulate insight fluently. Nothing shifted.

Only after she stepped away from a leadership role that conflicted with her values did her body respond. There was no dramatic exit. She simply stopped justifying why she stayed. Within weeks, her breath deepened. Her sleep stabilized. Her mind grew quieter without effort.

Truth did what strategy could not. The body does not respond to reassurance. It responds to congruence.

This understanding was deepened for me while writing *Stolen Memories: A Journey Through Alzheimer's*, where I witnessed again and again what remains when roles, cognition, and performance fall away. Presence. Truth. Relationship. The body, even in decline, remains honest.

## Coherence Simplifies without Shrinking

Many women fear that coherence will make life smaller. That fewer obligations will mean less relevance. That choosing alignment will require retreat.

In practice, coherence simplifies without diminishing.

One woman noticed this when she stopped attending gatherings that left her depleted, even though she had once been central in those spaces. She did not replace them with new commitments. She allowed space. What surprised her was not what disappeared, but what remained. Conversations deepened. Her presence carried more weight because it was no longer diluted. She spoke less often and was heard more clearly.

Her life did not contract. It clarified.

Relationships shifted as well. When she stopped

contradicting herself, others no longer had to navigate mixed signals. Boundaries became simpler. Some relationships deepened. Others completed their season. This was not loss. It was sorting.

## Coherence and Time

Earlier chapters explored urgency, pacing, and the reclamation of time. Coherence is what allows those changes to last.

One woman described coherence as no longer racing ahead of her life. She was still creating, still contributing, still engaged, but she was finally where she was. She noticed moments more fully. She finished conversations instead of rushing through them. Rest restored rather than merely compensating for exhaustion.

Time did not slow down. Resistance did. This understanding mirrors a core insight from *The Consciousness Blueprint*: presence does not require effort. It requires alignment. When inner conflict resolves, time becomes inhabitable.

## Coherence Is Responsive, Not Fixed

Living in coherence does not mean arriving at certainty and remaining there. It is not rigidity or perfection. It is responsiveness.

What aligns now may not align later. What fits today may require revision tomorrow. Coherence asks for listening rather than loyalty to outdated versions of yourself.

This is maturity. Coherence often replaces optimization. The question shifts from how I improve this to does this still belong. When the answer changes, coherence allows release without self-betrayal.

This is not a failure of commitment. It is fidelity to truth.

## A Bridge, Not an Ending

This book was never meant to tell you who to become.

It was meant to help you stop abandoning who you already are.

Living in coherence is the natural outcome of that return.

As you reach the close of this chapter and the end of this book, there is nothing left to master and nothing left to prove. There is only an invitation to notice when life feels settled inside you and to trust that sensation as guidance.

You may still grieve. You may still desire. You may still change your mind. Coherence does not remove complexity. It removes contradiction.

What follows is not a new identity, but a quieter relationship with yourself. One where effort aligns with meaning. Where rest is respected. Where love is chosen.

This is not the end of striving because striving was wrong. It is the end of striving that no longer serves.

What remains is presence. What remains is alignment. What remains is a life that no longer needs to argue with itself. That is coherence.

## Reflective Questions

1. Where in your life do you still feel pulled in opposing directions?

2. What situations require the most internal persuasion or self-negotiation?

3. How does your body respond when something feels aligned compared to when it does not?

4. What has simplified naturally as you have grown clearer about yourself?

5. Where are you still holding commitments that belong to an earlier version of you?

6. How does coherence show up for you as sensation rather than concept?

7. What would it mean to trust relief as a form of wisdom?

8.  How might your life feel if you no longer argued with yourself?

9.  What does coherence ask you to release now?

10. What does it invite you to remain faithful to?

216

# EPILOGUE:
# THE LIFE THAT WAS
# ALWAYS YOURS

There comes a quiet moment, often unannounced, when life stops asking who you have been and begins asking who you actually are now.

Not who you were expected to become. Not who you needed to be to succeed.

Not who you were required to be to belong.

But who you are when the noise settles, the roles loosen, and the proving is no longer necessary.

This book was never about reinvention. It was about remembering.

Remembering that aliveness is not reserved for the young.

That desire is not something to outgrow.

Emotionally mature power is steady, not loud.

That love deepens when it is chosen freely.

It was about honoring the truth that the second half of life is not a winding down – it is a refinement. A distillation. A season where clarity replaces urgency, presence replaces performance, and meaning replaces momentum.

If there is one quiet truth running through every chapter, it is this:

You do not owe the world your depletion.

You owe yourself honesty.

You owe your relationships presence.

You owe your future the freedom to choose wisely.

Whether you are a woman stepping fully into your seasoned self, or a man learning what it means to thrive beside one, the invitation is the same: alignment over appearance, depth over display, aliveness over accumulation.

The most fulfilled people in this season are not those

who did more.

They are those who listened sooner. Those who chose courage over compliance.

Those who allowed life to feel good again – without apology.

If you take anything from these pages, let it be permission.

Permission to want what you want. Permission to rest without guilt.

Permission to love without erasing yourself. Permission to choose a life that feels true, even if it looks different than expected.

The legacy you leave will not be measured by what you built alone, but by how you lived while building it.

Not by what you owned, but by what you embodied. Not by how busy you were, but by how awake you remained.

The art of living fully after success is not found in adding more chapters.

It is found in inhabiting the one you are in, completely.

This life, exactly as it is now, is not a prelude. It is not a waiting room. It is not the afterthought. It is life that was always yours.

And the most powerful choice you can make is to live it – present, aligned, and unapologetically alive.

With love and appreciation,

Maria L. Ellis, BBA, MBA

mellis@fsacap.com

# ACKNOWLEDGMENTS

No book is written alone, even when it is written in solitude.

This one carries the fingerprints of many conversations, quiet observations, courageous women, thoughtful men, and seasons of living that unfolded long before a single page was drafted.

To the women who trusted me with their stories, the ones shared over coffee, in boardrooms, in hospital waiting rooms, on long walks, and in unguarded pauses between responsibilities, thank you. Your honesty shaped these pages. Your willingness to name what felt invisible made this work possible.

To the men who listened, adapted, softened, and grew alongside the women in their lives, thank you for your openness. Emotional maturity is not loud, but it changes everything.

To my family, who have witnessed my becoming in real time, thank you for your patience during the quiet hours of reflection and the unseen labor behind each chapter. Your presence has been my grounding.

To the mentors, readers, and friends who challenged my thinking without dismissing it, thank you for refining my voice and sharpening my clarity.

To the earlier version of myself, the one who achieved, endured, and carried more than she needed to, thank you. Your effort created the conditions for this coherence.

And to the woman holding this book now:

Thank you for being willing to examine your life without condemnation.

Thank you for choosing honesty over performance.

Thank you for recognizing that strength does not require depletion.

If these pages offered language for what you already knew quietly, then they have done their work.

With love and appreciation,

Maria L. Ellis, BBA, MBA
mellis@fsacap.com

220

# SELECTED BIBLIOGRAPHY


Ellis, Maria L. *Stolen Memories: A Journey Through Alzheimer's.* Ellis Publishing House.

Ashe, Arthur. Quoted in various speeches and writings on resilience and personal agency.

Brown, Brené. *Dare to Lead.* Random House, 2018.

Brown, Brené. *The Gifts of Imperfection.* Hazelden Publishing, 2010.

Chopra, Deepak. *Ageless Body, Timeless Mind.* Harmony Books, 1993.

Chopra, Deepak. *The Seven Spiritual Laws of Success.* New World Library, 1994.

Frankl, Viktor E. *Man's Search for Meaning.* Beacon Press, 1946.

Goleman, Daniel. *Emotional Intelligence.* Bantam Books, 1995.

hooks, bell. *All About Love: New Visions.* William Morrow, 2000.

Kabat-Zinn, Jon. *Wherever You Go, There You Are.* Hyperion, 1994.

Neff, Kristin. *Self-Compassion.* William Morrow, 2011.

Palmer, Parker J. *Let Your Life Speak.* Jossey-Bass, 2000.

Palmer, Parker J. *On the Brink of Everything: Grace, Gravity, and Getting Old.* Berrett-Koehler Publishers, 2018.

Porges, Stephen W. *The Polyvagal Theory.* W.W. Norton & Company, 2011.

Rohr, Richard. *Falling Upward: A Spirituality for the Two Halves of Life.* Jossey-Bass, 2011.

Sandberg, Sheryl. *Lean In.* Knopf, 2013. (Referenced for cultural context around performance and achievement.)

Siegel, Daniel J. *The Developing Mind.* Guilford Press, 1999.

Tannen, Deborah. *You Just Don't Understand.* William

Morrow, 1990.

Whyte, David. *Consolations: The Solace, Nourishment and Underlying Meaning of Everyday Words*. Many Rivers Press, 2015.

Young, Tara Mohr. *Playing Big*. Avery, 2017.

# ABOUT THE AUTHOR

    Maria L. Ellis, BBA, MBA, is a life coach, educator, and multi-genre author whose work explores the intersection of leadership, longevity, feminine authority, and conscious living. After decades of professional success in banking, real estate, nonprofit leadership, and entrepreneurship, Maria turned her focus toward a deeper question: what does fulfillment look like after achievement?

    Her career began in corporate banking, where she worked with Fortune 500 companies financing international trade and advising business owners on financial strategy and legacy planning. Over the years, she expanded her work into real estate investment, leadership development, and educational advocacy, including more than twenty-five years promoting pay equity and opportunities for women and girls.

    Maria is also the author of over twelve books including Stolen Memories: A Journey Through Alzheimer's, a personal and clinical reflection on the impact of cognitive decline on families and identity. Across her writing, she blends lived experience with research, drawing from psychology, neuroscience, spiritual development, and the practical realities of modern life.

In her seventies, Maria continues to ski with her family, play golf by the ocean, mentor emerging leaders, and explore new technologies with curiosity rather than fear. Her work now centers on helping seasoned women move from performance to presence, from over-functioning to coherence, and from proving to embodying.

She believes that the second half of life is not a retreat from relevance, but an initiation into authorship.

Maria lives in Florida with her husband, surrounded by family, books, and the steady conviction that growth does not end, but refines.

# ABOUT ELLIS PUBLISHING HOUSE

Ellis Publishing House presents the work and vision of bestselling author and educator Maria L. Ellis, BBA, MBA. Founded to bring clear, useful ideas to a wide readership, the imprint focuses on practical nonfiction with enduring value – finance and business, health and longevity, leadership, caregiving, real estate, and poetry – alongside the signature *Journey to Wellness, Freedom, and Legacy* series. Editions are available in English and Spanish across print, eBook, and audio.

Maria's career spans international banking, investment advising, and financial planning, experience that informs her grounded approach to money, leadership, and long-term well-being. A graduate of the Harvard Business School Owner/President Management program, she holds business degrees from the University of Massachusetts Amherst and has served in leadership and advisory roles across education and nonprofit boards. Her books and talks emphasize clarity, compassion, and action – helping readers make better decisions for themselves, their families, and their communities.

Ellis Publishing House exists to advance that mission: books that translate expertise into everyday tools, invite thoughtful reflection, and encourage readers to build not only success but also significance. The catalog includes guides to financial freedom, family business legacy planning, entrepreneurial health, longevity, real-estate investing, leadership, caregiving, and a poetry collection that celebrates life on earth.

In all of its publishing, Ellis Publishing House favors ideas with measurable impact, stories with heart, and designs made to last – work shaped by Maria L. Ellis's commitment to service, integrity, and accessible excellence.

# OTHER BOOKS BY
# MARIA L. ELLIS, BBA, MBA

*Achieve Financial Freedom: The Road Map to Financial Success*

*Family Business Legacy Plan: The Ultimate Guide to Creating a Legacy for Your Family without Paying too Much in Taxes*

*Redefining Entrepreneurial Success: A Guide to a Healthy and Holistic Lifestyle*

*Longevity: Reinvent Yourself at Any Age*

*Life on Earth: Poetic Perspectives*

*Golf: A Course in Business: A Few Lessons Golf Can Teach Us About Management & Entrepreneurship*

*From Operator to Entrepreneur: Unlocking the Power of Visionary Leadership*

*Stolen Memories: A Journey Through Alzheimer's*

*Designing Your Longevity: A Personalized Blueprint for Thriving Longer with Energy, Purpose, and Vitality*

*Investing in Multifamily Real Estate: A Guide to Investing for Income, Impact, and Generational Wealth*

*Beyond Barriers: Women's Progress from Mid-Twentieth Century to Today*

*Life on Earth, Volume II: Poems That Inspire and Empower Women and Girls*

*The Consciousness Blueprint: Longevity, the Soul, and Humanity's Next Evolution*